THE NATURE AND VALUE OF HAPPINESS

THE NATURE
AND
VALUE OF HAPPINESS

CHRISTINE VITRANO

Foreword by Steven M. Cahn

WESTVIEW
PRESS

A Member of Perseus Books Group

Westview Press was founded in 1975 in Boulder, Colorado, by notable publisher and intellectual Fred Praeger. Westview Press continues to publish scholarly titles and high-quality undergraduate- and graduate-level textbooks in core social science disciplines. With books developed, written, and edited with the needs of serious nonfiction readers, professors, and students in mind, Westview Press honors its long history of publishing books that matter.

Published by Westview Press,
A Member of the Perseus Books Group

Find us on the World Wide Web at www.westviewpress.com.

Every effort has been made to secure required permissions for all text, images, maps, and other art reprinted in this volume.

Westview Press books are available at special discounts for bulk purchases in the United States by corporations, institutions, and other organizations. For more information, please contact the Special Markets Department at the Perseus Books Group, 2300 Chestnut Street, Suite 200, Philadelphia, PA 19103, or call (800) 810-4145, ext. 5000, or e-mail special.markets@perseusbooks.com.

Designed by Pauline Brown
Typeset in 11 point Adobe Garamond Pro

Library of Congress Cataloging-in-Publication Data

Vitrano, Christine.

The nature and value of happiness / Christine Vitrano.

    pages cm

Includes bibliographical references and index.

    ISBN 978-0-8133-4727-1 (pbk.) — ISBN 978-0-8133-4728-8 (e-book)
1. Happiness. I. Title.

B105.H36V58 2013

170—dc23

2012050399

10 9 8 7 6 5 4 3 2 1

For Julian and Gabriel, who have made me
happier than I ever could have imagined

CONTENTS

FOREWORD

Steven M. Cahn

What is happiness? How can it be achieved? Should attaining it be our ultimate goal? Might pursuing it ever conflict with our moral obligations?

These questions have been explored by philosophers since well over two millennia ago, when Socrates, then Plato, then Aristotle, then Epicurus strode the streets of Athens. And the issues have remained of concern throughout the centuries, discussed by such towering figures as Augustine, Aquinas, Hume, Kant, and Nietzsche, as well as leading philosophers of our own time. Indeed, as long as human life continues on earth, so probably will speculation about happiness.

Professor Vitrano has devoted many years to considering the numerous issues that surround happiness, and her understanding of the topic runs deep. Now, in this engaging book, she offers a remarkably lucid presentation of the subject, eschewing arcane terminology, obscure references, and convoluted arguments. She also illustrates her essential points with a host of illuminating examples.

I find her reasoning persuasive and her conclusions compelling. But even those who differ with her will appreciate the clarity of her style and her commitment to common sense.

In fact, reading her delightful book may even contribute to your happiness.

Introduction

Everyone wants to be happy, but if we ask the simple question "What is happiness?" something that seems so familiar, even obvious, suddenly becomes difficult to explain. More than two thousand years ago, the ancient Greeks inquired into the nature of happiness, and much of the work in the history of ethics is focused on answering their simple question: how can we live happy lives? Aristotle, for example, assumed that even if we have very different understandings of what happiness is and how we go about achieving it, everyone would agree that being happy is the key to living and doing well.

When I teach my class on happiness, I often begin the first lecture with a free association. I write the word *happiness* on the board and ask the class to share whatever comes to mind. My query is usually met with complete silence. Of course, I know my students have a lot to say about happiness, but I understand their initial hesitation. For all the familiarity of the word, most people recognize that happiness is a complicated concept, and no one wants to risk saying something foolish. After assuring the students that I am not seeking a formal definition, they often relax, and soon the entire board is filled with ideas connected in some way to happiness.

The point of this exercise is not to reach a consensus on how to define happiness, for we have the entire semester to accomplish that goal. Rather, I want my students to realize that they already possess key insights into the nature of happiness, even if their understanding is incomplete. Indeed, I believe we all have important intuitions about when a person is happy or unhappy, and these form the basis of our understanding of the term. These intuitions are useful when we analyze various philosophical views of happiness, and throughout this book, I shall appeal to these intuitions in order to assess particular theories of happiness.

When we examine the philosophical literature on happiness, we quickly note how little our struggles with this concept have changed in more than two thousand years. Although the rise of technology has improved many aspects of our lives, we are still grappling with the same questions posed by the ancient Greeks about how we should live and how we can achieve happiness. Recently, the work of philosophers has been eclipsed by empirically minded researchers in fields as diverse as psychology, sociology, and economics. Thus, research on happiness is no longer confined to academic journals, but rather frequently appears in newspaper and magazine articles. For example, psychologist Daniel Gilbert's book *The Pursuit of Happiness* was a national best seller, and Gilbert himself recently hosted a PBS special series entitled *This Emotional Life*.

I do not wish to downplay the importance of this empirical work on happiness, for it is interesting and sometimes even surprising.* I do wish, however, to emphasize the difference between the kinds of questions these empirical researchers ask and the questions that interest philosophers. Empirical researchers generally begin from the premise that the concept of happiness itself is something we already understand and is easily measured. Their studies typically look at the kinds of activities that promote or hinder happiness, which they often gauge using the subject's first-person reports of her satisfaction or dissatisfaction with her life. But this research begs the question against the philosopher, whose starting point is much more basic. In philosophy, we are not assuming we already have a clear understanding of happiness, for that is precisely why we are investigating the topic. Our goal is to answer questions relating to the nature and value of happiness, but providing answers to these kinds of questions requires a more theoretical approach.

One tradition in philosophy imposes artificial constraints on happiness, thereby distorting its meaning. Although the average person may not be able to present a formal definition of happiness that provides the conditions needed

---

* Perhaps my favorite surprising finding by psychologists is that having children does not actually increase happiness, but rather causes a dramatic decrease in happiness, from which the parents never fully recover until the children leave home (though I suppose parents of toddlers and teenagers already know that!).

to achieve it, she still has some understanding of what this term means, and I believe that commonsense view ought to constrain our philosophizing. We have a perfectly viable word in our lexicon—*happiness*—and it is adequate for the job it performs. Modifications of its meaning by philosophers are misleading and unnecessary if one is interested in explaining happiness, a notion employed by ordinary people.

In critically evaluating the different philosophical theories, I shall appeal to our commonsense intuitions about when a person is happy. Whenever a theory deviates from those intuitions—either by saying that a person is happy when our intuitions suggest that she is not or by saying she cannot be happy when our intuitions suggest that she is—I shall argue that we have serious reason to reject that view. The best theory will help us to understand the concept we commonly call "happiness," and it will not create a new concept.

This book will proceed by presenting and critically evaluating past and present philosophical theories of happiness, with each chapter focusing on one particular view. Some of the questions addressed include: How has our modern notion of happiness changed from its ancient origins? What is the precise value of happiness? Is happiness the greatest good or simply one good among many? Does being happy require one to be moral or to have a good life?

The first chapter will focus on hedonism, which identifies happiness with pleasure or with a strongly positive balance of pleasure over displeasure. Some theorists simply use the two words *happiness* and *pleasure* interchangeably, while others offer more extensive arguments as to why happiness and pleasure ought to be equated. But they all agree that *happiness* refers to a mental or psychological state of the individual, an account they believe is supported by common usage.

Our discussion will begin with the ancient philosopher Epicurus, who argues that all of our actions are directed toward happiness, which he identifies with pleasure. Epicurus rejects the typical hedonistic assumption that we should maximize the amount of pleasure we experience. Rather, he advocates moderation in our pursuit of pleasure, and he emphasizes the importance of reducing the amount of pain we experience so that we can achieve the ideal life of tranquillity. We shall also discuss two philosophers from the modern period, Jeremy Bentham and John Stuart Mill, whose utilitarian moral theory views happiness as the foundation of morality. Their "greatest happiness principle" directs us to maximize happiness whenever possible, and by happiness they mean simply pleasure and the absence of pain. Finally, we shall consider examples of contemporary philosophers who are hedonists about happiness.

Then we shall critically evaluate the hedonist's main thesis, which is that all instances of pleasure increase one's happiness and that all instances of pain decrease it. I shall raise several counterexamples that illustrate why this thesis is false and conclude that happiness must involve a more global attitude we have toward our lives. Although happiness is often affected by our experiences of pleasure and pain, it cannot be reduced to mere pleasure.

I have also included an appendix, which addresses the famous "Experience Machine" thought experiment posed by Robert Nozick. He argues that pleasure cannot be the key to living a happy life, because if there were a virtual reality machine into which one could plug that would provide nothing but pleasurable experiences of one's choosing, people would not plug in but would prefer to live in reality. In contrast to Nozick, I argue that many people would probably plug into the machine. But even if some people refuse, I suggest they may not do so for the reasons Nozick assumes. Instead, I conclude that Nozick's thought experiment does not actually present an objection to hedonism as a theory about happiness. However, given the other objections we have already discussed in Chapter 1, hedonism about happiness still ought to be rejected.

The second and third chapters will focus on the opposite view, which identifies happiness with virtue. The theorists in both of these chapters believe that happiness can be attained through a life of virtue or excellence, and this view is most closely associated with the ancient Greek and Roman moralists. Our discussion begins in Chapter 2 with Plato, who argues that having a just soul is both necessary and sufficient for achieving happiness. We shall consider Plato's view of justice, which he defines as the perfect balance of the different parts of one's soul, with each performing its distinct function. We shall also examine Plato's example of the just man who is unfairly persecuted by his society and put "up on the rack." According to Plato, despite all outward appearances, this man is happy, while an immoralist who appears to be flourishing is not.

Then we turn to the Stoics, who also identify happiness with virtue but define virtue in terms of living in accord with our essential rational nature. For the Stoic, one achieves happiness by recognizing the distinction between what is within our control (our own will and judgments) and what lies beyond our control (all external events) and by concerning ourselves only with what is within our control. The goal is to remain apathetic or emotionally unaffected by anything that happens that is beyond one's control, thus enabling one to preserve happiness regardless of what traumatic events one may face.

The third chapter begins with a discussion of Aristotle's view of happiness, which also emphasizes the importance of virtue. I shall argue that Aristotle's view is an improvement over the views of both Plato and the Stoics, because he also recognizes the importance of certain external goods, such as friendship, wealth, health, and luck. According to Aristotle, Plato's just man on the rack is not living a happy life, even though he is virtuous, for he lacks too many necessary external goods. I believe Aristotle's analysis of Plato's example is much closer to our commonsense judgments of when a person is happy.

The third chapter concludes with a critique of the view endorsed by Plato, the Stoics, and Aristotle, which identifies happiness with virtue. I shall raise several objections, the most pressing of which is that associating happiness with virtue deviates greatly from the way we use the word today. I suggest this view sets the bar for achieving happiness too high, and if we actually adopted this standard in our ordinary attributions of happiness, very few people would qualify as happy. I conclude that we should reject this conception of happiness.

The fourth chapter can be seen as an attempt to preserve the spirit of hedonism, but instead of identifying happiness with pleasure, these theorists identify it with the satisfaction of one's desires. I refer to this perspective as the "simple satisfaction view." The identification of happiness with getting what you want is prevalent within the contemporary literature, but this view of happiness is rarely justified by formal argument and is often stated as if it were indisputable.

I shall argue that the main weakness of associating happiness with desire satisfaction is that we don't always like what we want once we have it. I draw upon the empirical research on "affective forecasting" (which involves our inability to accurately predict future emotional states) to provide further justification for this objection, and I conclude that it is the subject's satisfaction (and not necessarily the desire for satisfaction) that actually correlates with happiness.

The fifth chapter can be seen as an amalgamation of the views in the second, third, and fourth chapters, for it combines the idea that happiness is a kind of satisfaction with the idea that happiness implies one is living a good life. The theorists in this chapter improve upon the theories I have already rejected by correctly identifying happiness with being in a state of satisfaction with one's life. But these theorists also wish to preserve the ancient moralists' intuition that being happy implies one is living the good life. To ensure the connection between happiness and goodness, these theorists view satisfaction as a necessary but not sufficient condition for being happy. They place a normative constraint on deeming someone happy.

I divide the theories in this chapter into two groups, based on the stringency of the standards they invoke in judging happiness. First, I consider the group with the most restrictive normative standards and show the incoherence of holding this view of happiness. Then I argue that even the more moderate evaluative view of happiness is indefensible. One problem with imposing normative constraints on happiness is that by permitting a third party to revert to her own values in judging other people's happiness, we turn happiness into an idiosyncratic concept that reveals nothing about the subject's own state of mind. According to this view, judgments of happiness become descriptions of the likes and dislikes of the third party who is making the judgments and do not reflect the subject or her values. But this approach deviates from the way we use the word *happiness,* and I argue that all of the normative theorists in this chapter are guilty of taking a word from the ordinary person's lexicon and providing it with a special philosophical meaning.

The sixth chapter focuses on the life-satisfaction view, which I shall argue is the most successful in capturing our ordinary understanding of happiness. I draw on the work of several contemporary theorists who believe happiness is nothing more than being satisfied with one's life, and I address several misconceptions people have about happiness. I also consider the question of whether happiness is a single concept and whether we can be mistaken about our own happiness. In the final section of this chapter, I discuss an objection raised by Daniel Haybron, who charges that judgments of life satisfaction are arbitrary. In response, I argue that Haybron's objection does not actually present a serious problem for the life-satisfaction view of happiness.

The seventh chapter focuses on the connection between happiness and morality. I defend the possibility that the immoralist can be happy, and I reply to the objections of two contemporary philosophers who deny this possibility.

Then I address the question of whether being moral or only appearing to be moral promotes a person's happiness, and I argue that merely appearing to be moral maximizes happiness.

Finally, the eighth chapter explores the practical implications of the life-satisfaction view of happiness, including what it implies about our ability to alleviate unhappiness and counsel others in their pursuit of happiness.

CHAPTER ONE

Happiness as Pleasure

The idea that happiness is nothing more than an experience of pleasure is called hedonism, a view that is popular today, but whose origin dates back to antiquity. Hedonists about happiness believe when we say that someone is happy, all we mean is that she has experienced pleasure (or, to be more technical, she has experienced a strongly positive balance of pleasure over displeasure). Some theorists simply use the two words *happiness* and *pleasure* interchangeably, while others offer more extensive arguments as to why they ought to be equated. But all hedonists agree that happiness is nothing more than a mental or psychological state of the individual, a state of pleasure, and they believe their view is supported by simply looking at the way we use the word *happy* in everyday conversation. Thomas Carson succinctly states the hedonists' main thesis about happiness: "All pleasures contribute to one's personal happiness whether or not they are good; similarly, all pains and unpleasant experiences detract from one's happiness irrespective of their value."[1]

Reflecting on ordinary usage, there does seem to be some support for hedonists' claim about the connection between happiness and pleasure, for we often use the words *happy* and *pleasant* synonymously. For example, when someone says that she is happy with her job, she often means that she generally enjoys her work or finds it pleasant. It would be very odd to hear someone say that she is happy with her job, but to insist that she detests being there or finds it absolutely dreadful or tedious. Alternatively, unhappy times in one's life are often marred by painful experiences, such as the loss of one's job or the death of a loved one. Furthermore, when you think of someone who is happy, you think of someone who feels good overall. Feeling good is simply a reference to one's mental or psychological state, and one reason people feel good is because they are experiencing pleasant moments or enjoyments. As Richard Campbell explains, a person who enjoys few or none of the activities in which she is engaged cannot possibly be leading a happy life, while the person who enjoys almost all of her activities cannot fail to achieve at least a minimum degree of happiness.[2] In contrast, unhappiness is often caused by painful experiences such as grief, despair, and depression, all of which are clearly experiences that we do not enjoy.

The Varieties of Hedonism

Hedonism about happiness should be distinguished from two other hedonistic doctrines with which it is often confused: ethical hedonism and psychological hedonism. Ethical hedonism is a theory of value, which views pleasure as the only thing that is intrinsically desirable and pain the only thing intrinsically undesirable. To say that something is intrinsically desirable is to say that we desire or value it solely for itself and not for any further reasons or consequences. For example, think about why someone undergoes a major surgery. One does not want to undergo surgery for its own intrinsic value; taken in itself, surgery is painful and onerous. But one agrees to the surgery, because it will (one hopes) lead to some beneficial consequences. Now think about the reason you desire something pleasurable, like eating chocolate cake (assuming you love chocolate as much as I do). You desire the pleasure of eating the cake for the experience itself—the intrinsic value of the pleasure is what motivates you.

Intrinsic value contrasts with instrumental value, which is when we value something for its good consequences (as in the surgery example). Money is a classic example of something that is valued instrumentally; in and of itself, money is nothing more than dirty paper. The value of money is instrumental, because it is directly connected to what we can do with it. Some things that we desire have both kinds of value. For instance, some people are runners, because they enjoy the experience of running (intrinsically) and because they value its good consequences (physical fitness). An art collector might value the pieces in her collection intrinsically (for their beauty) as well as instrumentally (for their monetary value).

Returning to ethical hedonism, one may think this view sounds like a mere platitude, for who would deny the intrinsic value of pleasure? Everyone wants to experience pleasure, even masochists, who derive pleasure from things ordinary people find painful. But ethical hedonism actually makes the bolder claim that pleasure is the *only* thing we value in and of itself. Ethical hedonism implies everything else that we desire is valuable *only* as a means to pleasure. So the ethical hedonist essentially reduces all value to one single source, which is pleasure.

Ethical hedonism is not a moral theory about which acts are morally right; nor does it tell us anything about our obligations to promote what is good. Rather, ethical hedonism is a theory of value that tells us which states of affairs are intrinsically good (those that produce pleasure). So you may choose to forego an experience of pleasure (like eating chocolate cake) and do something painful instead (like exercising) because you want to stay fit. Ethical hedonism does not imply you must always pursue pleasure and avoid pain, but it does imply that your life is good only insofar as it contains pleasure (and bad insofar as you experience pain).

The hedonist about happiness is not necessarily committed to ethical hedonism or to any particular views about the value or goodness of happiness. The hedonist about happiness would be an ethical hedonist only if she also held certain beliefs about the nature of happiness, namely, that happiness is the only thing that is intrinsically desirable. If one thought that happiness is the ultimate source of all intrinsic value, and one also thought that happiness is nothing more than a state of pleasure, then one would be committed to ethical hedonism.[3] But the hedonist about happiness need not take on such commitments, and I shall argue that she is better off rejecting ethical hedonism, because it is vulnerable to serious objections.

The first problem with ethical hedonism is that it deviates from our commonsense judgments about good and evil. As Richard Brandt notes, "Many people have at least thought either that some things other than pleasure are intrinsically good or that some kinds of pleasure are intrinsically bad. In the face of this, it is not easily claimed that 'intrinsically good' simply means pleasant."[4] To illustrate Brandt's point, think about someone who derives pleasure from witnessing another person's suffering. Ethical hedonism implies that all pleasure is intrinsically good, regardless of the source of that pleasure. But many people would argue that the pleasure derived from immoral acts like child molestation, rape, and torture is not intrinsically good.

One might also disagree with the ethical hedonist about pleasure being the sole source of intrinsic value, for there are many things people desire independent of pleasure. For example, philosophers have traditionally viewed knowledge, wisdom, and virtue as valuable even though they don't produce any pleasure. Parents might value loving and being loved by their children, but that value is often unrelated to pleasure (and as any parent can tell you, children are quite often a source of pain, yet we value being parents anyway). The hedonist about happiness can avoid these objections and recognize happiness as one good thing among many without viewing it as the sole source of intrinsic value.

Psychological hedonism, on the other hand, is an account of human motivation. Although there are several different varieties of psychological hedonism, what unites them according to Brandt is their belief that "actions or desires are determined by pleasures or displeasures, whether prospective, actual or past."[5] According to psychological hedonism, every time we act, we are motivated by pleasure, and we are always looking to maximize our overall experience of pleasure.

If the hedonist about happiness also accepted psychological hedonism, she would believe all our actions are aimed at maximizing happiness. One could certainly be a hedonist about happiness without viewing happiness as the driving force behind all our actions. I believe the hedonist about happiness should not endorse psychological hedonism, for as a theory of motivation, it appears to be false. People often act to promote the good of others at the expense of their own happiness. Consider the firefighter who enters a burning building or the woman who quits her job to move back home to care for her ailing parents. In both cases, their motivation is a sense of duty or moral obligation and not the promotion of their own happiness.

In response, the psychological hedonist could attempt to reinterpret these counterexamples as motivated by a desire to maximize happiness, but that move is implausible, because it is precisely their own happiness that is being sacrificed. However, even if psychological hedonism were a tenable view of human motivation, my point is that it is a distinct doctrine from hedonism about happiness.

What Is Pleasure?

One question we must address before delving further into hedonism is what do philosophers mean when they talk about pleasure? What is pleasure?

One promising strategy is to look at the way we classify other sensations. What is it that makes a particular sensation an itch or a tickle? What is it that all tickles have in common, such that we classify them as tickles (and not as some other sensation)? The answer is that we classify many sensations based on how they feel or how we experience them. All sensations of a particular kind feel more or less the same way, although they may differ in degree or in their felt intensity. Using this model, one might try to classify all pleasures the same way, based on how they feel.

But now we must ask: Is there one common feeling that occurs with each and every pleasant experience? And is this feeling what we use to identify that experience as a pleasure (as opposed to something else)?

Think about all the different sources of pleasure one might experience: some involve bodily sensations, whereas others involve our intellects. Some pleasures come from leisure and relaxation, while others are connected with physical exertion. Compare the pleasure one gets from reading an engrossing novel to the pleasure of swimming in the ocean. Some people take pleasure in playing sports like tennis or golf, whereas others find it in solving crossword puzzles. The problem is that each of these pleasant experiences feels very different. There does not seem to be one common feeling that occurs to unite them all, and so it cannot be in virtue of a feeling that we call them all pleasures.

Therefore, we need another strategy for describing what makes something a pleasure, and one place to start is with the dictionary. According to the *Oxford English Dictionary*, a pleasure is defined as "(1) The condition or sensation induced by the experience or anticipation of what is felt or viewed as good or desirable; enjoyment, delight; . . . and (2) A person's will, desire, or choice; that which is agreeable to one or in conformity with one's wish or will."[6] This definition provides an important key to classifying pleasures, for it suggests we define them by the attitude we take toward the experiences rather than by how they feel. This definition suggests we should classify pleasures as those experiences we enjoy or take delight in or that come from getting what we desire.

Henry Sidgwick rejects the view that all pleasures share a common feeling, and he is one of the first philosophers to suggest this alternative characterization. According to Sidgwick, what unites all of these states as pleasures is the favorable attitude we take toward them. As he explains, "When I reflect on the notion of pleasure . . . the only common quality that I can find in the feeling so designated seems to be that relation to desire . . . expressed by the general term 'desirable.' . . . I propose therefore to define Pleasure . . . as a feeling which, when experienced by intelligent beings, is at least implicitly apprehended as desirable or—in the cases of comparison—preferable."[7]

Although there is a considerable body of philosophical literature analyzing the concept of pleasure, Sidgwick's conception has influenced a number of prominent philosophers. For instance, Brandt defines a pleasant experience as one you wish "at the time to prolong (or in which one is absorbed without effort) for itself." In his article on hedonism in *The Encyclopedia of Philosophy*, Brandt elaborates on this view of pleasure: one is in a pleasant state of mind (or enjoying oneself) when "at the time he likes his experience or activity for itself, in the sense that, aside from moral considerations or considerations of consequences or of the possibility that something he likes even better could be substituted, he does not wish to change it and in fact would wish to avoid changing it if such a change impended."[8]

Fred Feldman refers to this Sidgwickian view as the dominant one within the literature, and he summarizes what these theories all have in common: "Each of them selects a certain attitude, A, and then maintains that a particular feeling is a pleasure (or is pleasant) on some occasion if and only if the person who experiences it takes up attitude A toward it on that occasion."[9] Given the agreement among philosophers, we shall rely mainly on this understanding of pleasure when we critically evaluate hedonism as a theory of happiness.

However, I would like to discuss one more interpretation, which is endorsed by Feldman, who has written extensively on hedonism. Although Feldman agrees that all pleasures do not share a common feeling, he offers a slightly different interpretation: rather than identifying pleasures with the experiences toward which we have a favorable attitude, Feldman identifies pleasure with the attitude itself. In Feldman's view, pleasures need not involve any sensory feelings at all, such as when you take pleasure in the fact that your stock port-folio is doing well, even though you are not presently feeling any sensations. As Feldman explains, "When we take pleasure in a state of affairs, we welcome it in a certain way; we are glad that it is happening; we like it in a certain familiar way."[10] We shall return to Feldman's view of pleasures and contrast it with the more typical understanding in the final section of this chapter, where we critically evaluate hedonism.

Now that we have seen what philosophers mean by *pleasure,* we shall review several historical accounts of hedonism about happiness. The first is from an ancient Greek ethicist, and the next two are from modern moral philosophers.

Ancient Hedonism

Epicurus lived during the Hellenistic period (from about 341 to 271 BCE), and he was a hedonist who believed the point of all our actions was to attain pleasure. However, Epicurus's understanding of pleasure is not typical, for he associates the pleasant life with tranquillity that is achieved through limiting your desires and ridding yourself of unnecessary fears. Epicurean hedonism should not be confused with the usual hedonist mantra "Eat, drink, and be merry," which conjures up images of jolly people at an endless banquet, con-suming copious amounts of food and wine. Epicurean hedonism, in contrast, is much more restrained, for Epicurus is keenly aware of the perils that come from indulging in too many physical or bodily pleasures. As he explains, "No pleasure is a bad thing in itself: but the means which produce some pleasures bring with them disturbances many times greater than the pleasures."[11]

Epicurus believes the intrinsic desirability of pleasure is both natural and apparent to us, for we immediately perceive the goodness of pleasure, just as we immediately perceive that fire is hot. As Terence Irwin explains, "Just as we follow the senses as guides to reality, so also we should follow our sensory affec-tions as guides to the good. Animals and children show us the natural tendency of our affections, before they are overlaid by misguided conventional beliefs about good and evil. If we attend to our affections, we recognize pleasure as the primary good, since it is the basis of all our natural conceptions of goodness, and as the ultimate good, since we aim at it in all our actions."[12] However, al-though all pleasures are intrinsically good, Epicurus does not believe all pleasures ought to be pursued (nor does he believe all pains should be avoided). Rather, we ought to consider what is in our long-term best interest and forego what will bring pleasure in the short run if doing so will ultimately lead to greater pleasure in the long run.[13]

Epicurus has a unique understanding of pleasure, for he rejects "the pleasures of profligates and those that consist in sensuality," preferring instead a state of tranquillity. Happiness cannot be achieved through indulging in the pleasures of continuous drinking, the satisfaction of lusts, or the enjoyment of luxuries, for these pursuits will more often bring one pain and suffering in the long run. Rather, Epicurus believes one achieves tranquillity by seeking "freedom from pain in the body and trouble in the mind." As Raymond Belliotti explains, "Epicurus' recipe for happiness was health, self-control, independence, moderation, simplicity, cheerfulness, friendship, prudence, intellectual and aesthetic values, and peace of mind. The calm, tranquil, harmonious life is the happy life."[14]

Epicurus was a hedonist about happiness, but the question of whether he also endorsed ethical and psychological hedonism is a contested one among scholars. Richard Taylor, for example, views Epicurus as an ethical hedonist, who believes pleasure is the only ultimate good and the only thing we desire solely for its intrinsic value. According to Taylor, even friendship and virtue, which Epicurus viewed as essential for living a happy life, are valued not intrinsically, but only instrumentally as a means to living a pleasant, tranquil life.[15] As Taylor explains, "This philosophy, then, is no philosophy of heroic deeds. It is self-regarding throughout, and even the virtue of friendship, upon which the Epicureans placed so much stress, is recommended solely for its rewards to oneself; you are not expected to love friends for their sake, but for your own."[16]

Terence Irwin offers a similar interpretation, for he argues that Epicurus is opposed to the idea that virtue and friendship are intrinsically (noninstrumentally) good. According to Irwin, Plato and Aristotle accept the following argument against hedonism: if virtue is noninstrumentally valuable, hedonism is false; virtue is noninstrumentally good; hedonism is false. Irwin argues that Epicurus agrees with the first premise but rejects the second, for he views virtuous action as a source of pleasure, and this pleasure is what makes virtue good. As Irwin explains, virtues "are sources of pleasure in a purely causal sense, by producing results that are pleasant in themselves or instrumental to such results."[17]

However, Julia Annas offers a very different interpretation of Epicurus's view of virtue and friendship, for Annas believes Epicurus's view can accommodate the intrinsic (noninstrumental) value of the virtues and friendship. As Annas explains, "Epicurus is expanding the notion of pleasure . . . so that living virtuously is part of what living pleasantly is. . . . So pleasure, at least the kind that forms our final end, must be the kind of thing which can include everything that we seek for its own sake. And so it must include, in some way, living virtuously, since this is something we seek for its own sake. It must also include friendship. For having a friend is like living virtuously—it is something we do for its own sake." Therefore, although we engage in friendships because of the pleasure they produce, "this does not lead to selfishness, or to viewing friendship instrumentally; for pleasure as our final end has been expanded to include the pleasure from genuine other-concern. The argument is, as the Epicureans saw, exactly the same as with the virtues; the pleasure we seek is expanded so that we achieve it precisely by having non-instrumental concern for virtuous action and the interests of others." Annas also argues that pleasure and the virtues are mutually entailing, because "having the virtues entails getting pleasure from them" and "living pleasantly entails having the virtues."[18]

According to Epicurus, the main source of our unhappiness is pain that arises from fear. So the key to living a happy life is to rid ourselves of unnecessary fears. Epicurus discusses three sources of fear that he believes are within our control to reduce or eliminate: fear of the gods, fear of death, and anxiety over the future.

Starting with the first source of fear, Epicurus reasons that we should not fear the gods, because they have no awareness of our existence and no concern for us. Epicurus reaches this conclusion by reflecting on the problem of evil, which is the problem of how an omnipotent, omniscient, benevolent God could exist when there is so much evil in the world. Some people respond to the problem of evil by simply denying the existence of God, but Epicurus thought we had knowledge of the gods "by clear vision" as immortal, supremely blessed, and happy beings.[19] But our conception of the gods as happy and blessed is not consistent with their caring about human beings or being aware of the miseries in the world. Epicurus resolves this inconsistency by denying divine Providence, which is the belief that God is actively involved in the world. Instead, Epicurus argues, the gods live eternally in another place with no direct knowledge of us, and they should function as ethical ideals that we need not fear.

Moving on to the second source of fear, Epicurus advises, "The wise man neither seeks to escape life nor fears the cessation of life, for neither does life offend him nor does the absence of life seem to be any evil. And just as with food he does not seek simply the larger share and nothing else, but rather the most pleasant, so he seeks to enjoy not the longest period of time, but the most pleasant." Epicurus believed that all good and evil consist in sensations of pleasure and pain. But death (by definition) is the deprivation of sensation; when we are dead, we cannot feel anything. Therefore, death cannot cause us any harm, and, therefore, it gives us no reason for fear. Epicurus explains this argument succinctly: "So death, the most terrifying of ills, is nothing to us, since so long as we exist, death is not with us; but when death comes, then we do not exist."[20]

Epicurus also offers the symmetry argument for why we should not fear death: consider the infinity of time that occurred before you were born. This prenatal past infinity is no different from the future infinity that will occur after you die, yet few people are troubled by what has occurred before they were born. But if your prenatal nonexistence does not disturb you, Epicurus argues, neither should your postmortem nonexistence, since they are not significantly different.[21]

The final source of pain arises from our anxiety about the future, and whether we will be able to continue to satisfy our desires. Epicurus believes that our desires play a key role in living happily, for they are a source of both pleasure (when satisfied) and pain (when frustrated). If satisfying our desires causes pleasure, one might assume a hedonist would advise us to satisfy as many desires as possible, thereby maximizing our experience of pleasure. Epicurus suggests this approach with desires he refers to as "natural and necessary," such as the desire for food, water, and shelter from the environment. These desires are vital for our survival, and produce a lot of pain when frustrated. Since they are naturally limited and relatively easy to fulfill, Epicurus says that we should try to satisfy them whenever we can.

However, we also have desires for things we enjoy that are not necessary for our survival, such as vacations to Europe, eating in expensive restaurants, and owning designer handbags. Epicurus refers to these desires as "natural but non-necessary," for they refer to indulgences. Besides being difficult to satisfy, these desires are problematic, because they have no natural limit. Satisfying these desires may provide pleasure, but they also raise our expectations, thereby increasing the pressure to continue satisfying them.[22] Similar problems arise with what Epicurus refers to as vain desires, which include the desire for fame, power, and wealth. Vain desires are also limitless, for one can never be content with any amount of power, fame, or money. Rather than struggling to satisfy these nonnecessary and vain desires, Epicurus suggests that we should simply eliminate them, for he believes paring down our desires to the most basic necessities is the only way to achieve contentment. As he explains, "If you wish to make Pythocles wealthy, don't give him more money; rather, reduce his desires."[23]

Putting all of this together, Epicurus's strategy for achieving happiness involves avoiding unnecessary pain (from our fear of the gods, death, and frustration of our desires) and enjoying the simple pleasures that come from satisfying our necessary desires. The lifestyle Epicurus recommends is quite ascetic, and his strategies for achieving happiness are focused on pain avoidance rather than pleasure enhancement. But Epicurus believed an ascetic life could still bring one pleasure. As he explains, "Plain savours bring us a pleasure equal to a luxurious diet, when all the pain due to want is removed; and bread and water produce the highest pleasure, when one who needs them puts them to his lips. To grow accustomed therefore to a simple and not luxurious diet gives us health to the full, and makes a man alert for the needful employments of life."[24]

Recent empirical work on happiness supports some of Epicurus's claims about how we achieve happiness. For instance, although living standards have more than doubled in the past fifty years in the United States, and there have been massive increases in real income at every point of the income distribution, the percentage of people who describe themselves as "happy" has not changed since the 1950s, and according to some surveys, Americans have become somewhat less satisfied with their lives over the past thirty years.[25] Worse still, depression rates, which indicate national unhappiness, have steadily risen with our rising prosperity. Despite the fact that America has become an increasingly wealthy country, and ordinary people can now afford many luxuries that were once reserved solely for the wealthy, the data show we are not any happier for these advances.

Gregg Easterbrook refers to this phenomenon as "the progress paradox": since the end of World War II, "per-capita income, 'real' income, longevity, home size, cars per driver, phone calls made annually, trips taken annually, highest degree earned, IQ scores, just about every objective indicator of social welfare has trended upward on a pretty much uninterrupted basis for two generations. . . . [But] the trend line for happiness has been flat for fifty years. The trend line is negative for the number of people who consider themselves 'very happy,' that percentage gradually declining since the 1940's. . . . Adjusting for population growth, ten times as many people in the Western nations today suffer from 'unipolar' depression, or unremitting bad feelings without a specific cause, than did a half century ago. Americans . . . have ever more of everything except happiness."[26]

Other studies have found a positive correlation between the quality of our personal relationships and happiness. Epicurus emphasizes the importance of friendship, which he views as essential for living a tranquil life. As he explains, "Of all the things which wisdom acquires to produce the blessedness of the complete life, far the greatest is the possession of friendship."[27] In surveys 85 percent of Americans say they wish they could spend more time with their families, and studies show that among rich countries, people in the United States work the longest hours, particularly when compared with people in Europe. Yet the happiness of Americans has stagnated since 1975, whereas it has steadily risen in Europe.[28] Americans appear to be trapped in a cycle of earning money to afford luxuries, which then force us to earn even more to maintain our lifestyles. The problem is that satisfying our nonnecessary desires is not making us any happier. Epicurus would advise us to stop fighting this losing battle with our desires and eliminate them instead. By reducing our dependence on luxuries, we will be able to work less and focus more on doing the things we actually enjoy, like spending time with our friends and families.

Modern Hedonism

Jeremy Bentham and John Stuart Mill were two prominent moral philosophers from the modern era (which spans from the seventeenth to the early twentieth centuries) who identify happiness with pleasure. Bentham and Mill both endorse utilitarianism, the moral theory that views happiness as the foundation of morality. In order to fully understand their views on happiness, some background on utilitarianism will be helpful. Put simply, utilitarians believe an act is morally right if it maximizes the happiness (or pleasure) of everyone affected by that act. Utilitarians believe the consequences of an act determine its moral value. They look at the total happiness produced by each possible course of action, where the total happiness is simply a tally of the happiness (or unhappiness) of each person affected by that action. Utilitarians believe the act that produces the most happiness (or the least unhappiness) is the one that ought to be done.

Starting with Bentham's view of happiness, which is the simpler of the two, he says that being happy is nothing more than being in the right mental state, namely, one of pleasure and not pain. As Bentham explains, "Nature has placed mankind under the governance of two sovereign masters, *pain* and *pleasure*. It is for them alone to point out what we ought to do, as well as to determine what we shall do. On the one hand the standard of right and wrong, on the other the chain of causes and effects, are fastened to their throne."[29] From this quote, we can see Bentham endorses both ethical and psychological hedonism in addition to utilitarianism. He views pleasure as the ultimate motive behind all our actions, as well as the measure of good and evil, right and wrong.

Bentham believes all pleasures are sensations that are alike in quality and differ only in quantity. Because all pleasures are alike in quality, Bentham views all pleasures as good, regardless of their source. Bentham presents a "hedonic calculus," which is a list of criteria to consider when we evaluate the total pleasure produced by any action. Bentham believes we can assign a numerical value to the pleasure produced by every act, thereby enabling us to compare them. The criteria in his hedonic calculus list the different quantitative dimensions of pleasures, which include their intensity, duration, and the certainty we have that an act will produce pleasure. Bentham's hedonic calculus also has us consider the likelihood that a sensation will (or will not) be followed by more pleasure. So one might choose a pleasure that is less intense, because it is more certain and will last longer, as when one chooses to save money rather than spend it on lottery tickets. One might also endure short-term pains in order to achieve a long-term pleasure, such as suffering through medical school in order to achieve one's dream of becoming a doctor.

Let's consider an example to see how to apply Bentham's hedonic calculus. Suppose my sister must move out of her apartment this weekend, and I have reluctantly agreed to help her despite my hatred of lifting anything heavy. My problem is that a friend has just invited me to her beach house for the weekend, and I cannot go if I help my sister move. Morally speaking, what does the utilitarian say I should do?

According to utilitarianism, I should look at the total happiness produced by each possibility. Keeping in mind the criteria in Bentham's calculus, I can assign a numerical value to the happiness (pleasure) of each person affected. To keep things simple, let's assume the only two people affected are my sister and myself. In the first scenario, I decide to keep my promise: I help my sister move, she is eternally grateful, and although I am slightly bitter about missing out on the beach, I feel good about helping her. In this scenario, my sister's happiness is increased by +10 units of pleasure, and my happiness is increased by +1 unit of pleasure. In the second scenario, I renege on my promise, my sister is absolutely furious, and I have trouble enjoying my time at the beach, because I feel guilty about upsetting my sister. In this scenario, my sister's happiness decreases by −10 units of pleasure, while mine increases by +3 units of pleasure. If we compare the total happiness produced in each scenario (+11 units of pleasure in the first versus −7 units of pleasure in the second), the utilitarian would say that I ought to help my sister move, because that will result in the most happiness overall.

Bentham views all pleasures as alike in quality, and he does not believe pleasures related to the intellect are superior to those related to the body. Viewing all pleasures as equal in quality implies that the pleasure one gets from reading a novel, writing poetry, or playing a musical instrument is no different in nature (or kind) from the pleasure one gets from gossiping with friends, receiving a massage, or using drugs. Some critics find this implication of utilitarianism disturbing, for it implies that activities that are base, degrading, or shallow will receive the same moral consideration as activities that encourage us to cultivate our minds and develop our talents. Some have objected to utilitarianism on the grounds that it debases human beings by implying human life has no higher or nobler purpose than the pursuit of pleasure. This theory, they charge, is fit for a swine or any other animal, but not for a human being.[30]

Mill responds to these charges by reminding us this is the same attack launched against the Epicureans, who had a simple but clever reply. Following the Epicureans, Mill argues that it is the objector who reduces human life to that of a swine, for the objector is assuming human beings are not capable of any greater pleasure than that of an animal. But human beings can clearly enjoy many experiences animals are incapable of appreciating, for we have higher cognitive abilities. Although our intellects make it more difficult for us to achieve happiness, Mill argues that no human being would ever be willing to give them up, for "in spite of these liabilities, he can never really wish to sink into what he feels to be a lower grade of existence." As Mill explains, "No intelligent human being would consent to be a fool, no instructed person would be an ignoramus, no person of feeling and conscience would be selfish and base, even though they should be persuaded that the fool, the dunce, or the rascal is better satisfied with his lot than they are with theirs."[31]

Mill also argues there are intrinsic differences between pleasures that render some pleasures more valuable than others. All pleasures are not equal, Mill declares, and the utilitarian's calculations should factor in differences in quality as well as quantity. Mill suggests that pleasures of the intellect, which use our distinctively human higher faculties, are better than pleasures that arise from bodily sensations. When trying to determine whether a pleasure is higher or lower, we should ask ourselves whether it is a pleasure an animal could also appreciate; if not, then it is probably a higher pleasure. Examples of higher pleasures include activities such as doing philosophy, creating a work of art, or playing a musical instrument. Lower pleasures include the bodily sensations you might experience when eating, drinking, or having sex. Mill's advice for distinguishing between higher and lower pleasures is to appeal to someone who has experienced both, for he argues no person who has experienced both would be willing to trade a higher pleasure for any amount of the lower, even if the higher is more difficult to obtain. As Mill explains, "It is better to be a human being dissatisfied than a pig satisfied; better to be Socrates dissatisfied than a fool satisfied. And if the fool or the pig are of a different opinion, it is because they only know their own side of the question. The other party to the comparison knows both sides."[32]

Mill believes our possession of higher faculties is the source of our pride, our love of liberty and independence, and, most important, our sense of dignity. He believes the cultivation of our higher faculties enables us to appreciate a seemingly endless world of enjoyments that include everything from an appreciation of the natural world to learning about the history of mankind. As he explains, "In a world in which there is so much to interest, so much to enjoy, and so much also to correct and improve, everyone who has this moderate amount of moral and intellectual requisites is capable of an existence which may be called enviable."[33]

Contemporary Hedonism

Although hedonism has largely fallen out of favor among contemporary theorists, we shall focus on two philosophers who support hedonism. Wayne Davis draws a distinction between what he calls the occurrent and the dispositional senses of happiness.[34] According to Davis, one is occurrently happy if she is presently experiencing or feeling happiness, which is evident because she is smiling, she feels good, or she is in good spirits. Davis identifies occurrent happiness with pleasure. Dispositional happiness occurs when one is predominately happy in the occurrent sense, meaning one often feels happy. Being dispositionally happy implies that one is living a happy life. Davis argues that simply experiencing occurrent happiness is not sufficient for being dispositionally happy, because a homeless person can enjoy the momentary pleasure of drinking a cup of coffee, but that does not mean he is living a happy life. Alternatively, one can be dispositionally happy even though one is not experiencing occurrent happiness. You may be occurrently unhappy when you get a flat tire, but that one incident is not enough to cause you to live an unhappy life. However, Davis is committed to the idea that living a happy life is nothing more than having mostly pleasant experiences, and the more pleasure one experiences, the happier her life will be.

Another contemporary philosopher, Fred Feldman, presents what he calls an attitudinal version of hedonism, which views pleasures as "pro- attitudes" we take toward things. To say that someone is experiencing attitudinal pleasure is akin to saying that she "enjoys it, is pleased about it, is glad that it is happening, is delighted by it."[35] Therefore, in Feldman's view, a person's happiness at a particular moment is equivalent to the amount of attitudinal pleasure that she takes in things at that time minus the amount of attitudinal displeasure she takes in things at that time. Put simply, "to be happy at a moment is to be taking more pleasure than displeasure in things at that moment."[36]

We have now reviewed three historical examples of hedonism as well as two contemporary accounts, and we are ready to evaluate whether this view is a viable theory of happiness.

Should We Be Hedonists About Happiness?

We can begin with Carson's statement of the hedonist's main thesis: "All pleasures contribute to one's personal happiness, and all pains and unpleasant experiences detract from one's happiness."[37] The two main lines of attack I shall initially pursue involve examples in which people are experiencing pleasure without increased levels of happiness (or even with an increase in unhappiness) and examples of people increasing their happiness without experiencing an increase in pleasure (or even with an increase of pain or displeasure).

The first example contradicts the hedonist's thesis by showing that all pleasures do not contribute to happiness. Ordinarily, eating chocolate cake is a very enjoyable experience for me. The act of eating the cake is a pleasure, because it is an experience toward which I have a favorable attitude: I like the experience, and I always wish to prolong it, whenever I allow myself to indulge. However, I have just started a new diet, and I am trying hard to improve my eating habits. My goal is to lose a significant amount of weight and adopt a healthier lifestyle. Unfortunately, this lifestyle does not include eating chocolate cake. If I indulge in the pleasant experience of eating the cake, I shall become unhappy and regret not having more willpower. The experience of eating the cake will not be different; the taste will be just as appealing and enjoyable. Yet the pleasure will lead not to happiness, but to unhappiness instead. If I resist the temptation to eat the cake and deny myself the experience of pleasure, I will be happy, because I will be successfully working toward my weight-loss goal. This example suggests my happiness is completely independent of any experience of pleasure. In this case, it is actually the denial of pleasure that promotes my happiness.

Furthermore, the act of restraint is, in itself, an unpleasant experience. I wish I could eat the cake, especially when I see everyone else enjoying it. The hedonistic thesis says this unpleasant experience should decrease my happiness, yet it does not; it contributes to my happiness instead. Therefore, happy mental states cannot be identical with (or reduced to) pleasant states, because many pleasurable experiences do not contribute to happiness and some unpleasant ones do.

Hedonism about happiness is far too simplistic, for a person's happiness is more complex than just an occurrent mental state one enjoys or wishes to prolong. Happiness appears to involve a more global attitude one has toward her life, an attitude that takes into consideration how one's immediate experiences fit into her life as a whole. Although this attitude may be (and often is) influenced by pleasant or unpleasant experiences, it cannot be identified with such immediate experiences.

Another example illustrates this point. Suppose a person participates in a golf tournament in which she is greatly outmatched by the other competitors, and she ends up finishing in last place. The experience of losing is itself rather unpleasant, yet it does not make her unhappy. Losing doesn't even decrease her happiness significantly, for she had no expectation of winning. She feels quite satisfied with her performance and is glad she tried to compete. Although the experience of losing was unpleasant, she remains happy just the same.

Happiness and pleasure are also intuitively different. With sensory pleasures, we aim at the experience itself; we eat the ice cream because of the sensations we feel. Happiness is a deeper emotion that goes beyond the immediate sensory experience. We are made happy by events that are of some significance to us, whereas events that have little or no significance can still be pleasant. For example, my happiness when you give me roses differs from the pleasure I get from smelling them. The pleasure is an immediate sensory experience that I enjoy, whereas the feeling of happiness results from my perception that you care for me. Daniel Haybron discusses a related problem, which is that hedonism is too inclusive, for it counts all sorts of fleeting, trivial pleasures as contributing to happiness. Yet, as Haybron notes, there are many enjoyments such as "eating crackers, hearing a good song, sexual intercourse, scratching an itch, solving a puzzle, [and] playing football" that may not have the slightest impact on one's level of happiness.[38]

L. W. Sumner makes a related point about the nature of pain, which helps to explain the temptation to adopt a hedonistic conception of happiness. Sumner notes that "pain is typically, though not necessarily, accompanied by feelings of fear, anxiety, anger, indignity, depression or despair."[39] The ordinary use of *happy* is incompatible with these negative feelings, whereas pleasures are typically associated with positive feelings. If pains cause feelings that annihilate happiness, one may be tempted to conclude that pleasures must produce happiness, or that happiness is equivalent to pleasure and the absence of pain. The main problem with this assumption is that our common usage of *happy* permits attributions of happiness in the absence of pleasure and in the presence of pain, so the two terms cannot be identical.

Consider another example. Debbie has recently learned that she is pregnant. After trying to conceive for nearly a year, she had almost given up hope of having a child. Now she is ecstatic over the news that she will be a mother. Debbie suffers from severe morning sickness that leaves her virtually immobile most mornings. This experience of nausea and dizziness plagues her for months; she is often unable to eat and feels uncomfortable most of the time. To say that she is not enjoying her pregnancy is an understatement, and she often feels utterly miserable. Although this pregnancy is quite unpleasant and even painful at times, she has never been happier in her life. More important, calling her happy is appropriate and entirely in accord with our ordinary usage of the word.

In other cases, people are willing to make considerable sacrifices for their loved ones, such as undergoing major surgery in order to donate vital organs. Besides the risks associated with any major surgery, the donor often faces considerable recovery time, which may be quite painful. Must we assume, on that basis, that the donor is unhappy or that she would have been much happier had she not undergone the surgery? The donor was certainly warned about the risks beforehand, yet she still agreed to undergo the procedure. One reason is that the donor is made happy by the thought that she is able to save her loved one's life. Nothing is contradictory about describing the organ donor as happy, despite the considerable pain and anxiety she experiences.

Haybron raises another important objection to hedonism, which is that it makes happiness an "essentially episodic and backward-looking phenomenon."[40] All hedonistic happiness can inform us about are the kinds of experiences the subject has already had. It offers us no picture into the future and no assurance of stability. The hedonistic view of happiness misrepresents the function of our ordinary concept of happiness, which does tell us something about that person's view of her life and current mood. Knowing that someone is happy tells us how she is feeling now, but it also provides some insight into her immediate future. If one knew about an impending doom, one probably wouldn't be happy right now; she'd be worried about the future. Yet pleasure functions in exactly the opposite way. To know that someone has recently experienced something enjoyable tells us nothing about her present or future experience, but only about her past.

Knowing that a person is happy also enables us to make certain behavioral predictions that we could not make based on knowledge of her experiences of pleasure. If I know that you are happy about a promotion you received at work, then I can expect you to be in a good mood when I see you. I certainly don't expect you to come home dour and depressed. Alternatively, if your son is flunking out of school, and I know how much you value education, I can expect you to be unhappy upon hearing the news of his failure. People are made happy or unhappy by significant events in their lives. In many cases, their happiness is not due to the presence (or absence) of pleasurable experiences. Knowing that you had a good meal last night or a massage today does not warrant any assumptions about your current mood or state of mind. As Haybron notes, happiness "tells us not just about subjects' histories, but also about their current condition and propensities for the near future. It is forward-looking."[41] Therefore, the hedonistic view misrepresents our ordinary concept of happiness.

Perhaps the hedonist can offer a reply to our objections by appealing to the other interpretation of pleasure we discussed earlier, which came from Feldman. The hedonist might argue that the counterexamples I have presented show only the inadequacy of what we might call "sensory hedonism," the view found in Epicurus, Bentham, and Mill, which is restated by Carson. But perhaps someone like Feldman, who endorses "attitudinal hedonism," can escape these objections. In Feldman's view, pleasures are not sensations or feelings but "pro- attitudes" that we take toward things. To say that someone is experiencing attitudinal pleasure is like saying she is "pleased about something" or she "takes pleasure in some state of affairs." Feldman also describes attitudinal pleasure as akin to saying that someone "enjoys it, is pleased about it, is glad that it is happening, is delighted by it."[42]

The hedonist might object that my examples involving chocolate cake and the woman experiencing morning sickness do not pose a problem for the attitudinal hedonist, because the attitudinal pleasure you experience in these cases will reflect your values or what is important to you and not merely the enjoyable or unenjoyable sensations you are experiencing. For instance, if you value sticking with your diet, then you would *not* have a positive attitude toward eating the chocolate cake. So the attitudinal hedonist reaches the correct verdict in this case: eating the cake does not contribute to your happiness. Similar reasoning applies to the woman experiencing morning sickness: although her pregnancy is painful, she has a strong desire to have a child and views the pregnancy favorably. So the attitudinal hedonist would count being pregnant as an attitudinal pleasure that contributes to her happiness.

In response, I would argue that attitudinal hedonism is still objectionable, because there are a multitude of things about which I am attitudinally pleased (or displeased) that have absolutely no impact on my happiness. Consider several examples: I might be pleased to see prodemocracy rallies in Africa and the Middle East, even though I have no close friends of relatives who live there. I might enjoy reading about the impeachment of a corrupt politician, even though he is from another state or even another country. I might even be glad to learn that Brazil will be hosting the World Cup in 2014, even though I have no interest in soccer and no personal ties to Brazil. Although I might experience "attitudinal pleasure" in all of these cases, it is quite plausible that none of these instances will have any influence on my present level of happiness. The problem is that attitudinal hedonism casts the net far too wide, for it counts each and every positive attitude as contributing toward a person's present level of happiness. But a person can have a positive attitude toward many things that are not important, valuable, or significant enough to affect her happiness. Perhaps I am pleased about the prodemocracy rallies because I believe democracy is a superior form of government. If I have no personal connection to anyone in that area, why should we assume that attitude also increases my level of happiness?

Consider all the stories one encounters each day in newspapers, on television, and from various online sources. Many of these stories will elicit from you an emotional reaction that is either positive or negative. Is it really plausible to say that each of these emotionally engaging stories also had an impact on your level of happiness? This implication seems especially bizarre when we consider all the trivial, meaningless events that might inspire a positive attitude, such as the breakup of a celebrity couple or a performance by Lady Gaga at the Grammy Awards.

The problem for attitudinal hedonism gets even more serious when we consider the emotional reactions that are inspired by fictitious characters in television shows, movies, and novels. We can't help but get emotionally invested in these forms of entertainment, where we literally "feel" for the characters. It seems natural to say one is glad when something good happens to a character one likes or that one takes delight in seeing the "bad guys" get what they deserve. Although works of fiction can elicit empathic responses from us, I don't think anyone would say their personal level of happiness is thereby affected.

Consider one more example: I recently read about a horrific case of child abuse, and I found this case especially disturbing because it involved a little boy about the same age as my son. Although I experienced a significant amount of "attitudinal displeasure" while reading this story, it did not affect my level of happiness. This boy's tragic story, although extremely unpleasant to read about, has no bearing on me or my loved ones. There are a lot of things happening in the world that I dislike, but only a small portion of these events will actually have an impact on my level of happiness. Although hedonists are right that happiness involves experiencing positive attitudes, their mistake is to count *every* positive attitude as contributing to happiness and *every* negative one as reducing it.

If so many objections to hedonism can be found, one might wonder why hedonism has been endorsed by such prominent thinkers throughout the history of philosophy. One reason hedonism is attractive is because it makes happiness easy to quantify, and for the utilitarians (who identify the morally right act as the one that produces the most happiness) quantification is important. As Taylor explains, some philosophers "want to think of happiness as something familiar, identifiable, and even measurable, rather than as something problematical or dubious. Pleasure, being an actual and common feeling, is certainly familiar and identifiable, and there seems to be no reason in principle why it should not be measurable."[43]

Hedonism is also appealing because it emphasizes the importance of enjoyment in a happy life. Consider a person who derives no enjoyment from her daily activities, who dreads waking up in the morning because she finds her life to be tedious and burdensome. One pictures this woman as miserable or dejected; one could not describe her as happy. Clinical depression is defined as an ahedonic state, meaning the depressed person cannot derive pleasure from any of the activities she usually enjoys. If depression (which is clearly a state of unhappiness) is defined in terms of an inability to experience pleasure, it seems natural to equate happiness with the opposite, namely, pleasure. The problem is that a person's happiness is more complex than simply totaling up her experiences of pleasure and subtracting her experiences of pain. As all of the counterexamples show, some instances of pleasure do not contribute to happiness, while some instances of pain do.

Although we should reject the hedonists' account of happiness, we should take note of the things the hedonist does get right. She is talking about the right subject matter, for happiness is a mental state that is often influenced by one's experiences of pleasure and pain and one's positive and negative attitudes. The hedonist's mistake is to reduce happiness to the experience of pleasure, when happiness appears to be a more complex phenomenon.

In the next two chapters, we shall consider another view of happiness that originated with the ancient Greek moralists and is still popular today, which is the view that identifies happiness with virtue.

Notes

1. Thomas Carson, "Happiness and the Good Life," *Southwestern Journal of Philosophy* 9 (1978): 78.

2. Richard Campbell, "The Pursuit of Happiness," *Personalist* (1973): 325–337.

3. The view that happiness is the sole source of intrinsic value was quite popular among the ancient Greek philosophers, many of whom viewed happiness as the end goal or purpose of life. I shall discuss this view of happiness in Chapters 2 and 3, where I address the connection between happiness and virtue.

4. Richard Brandt, "Hedonism," in *The Encyclopedia of Philosophy*, edited by P. Edwards (New York: Macmillan, 1967), 434.

5. Ibid., 433.

6. *New Shorter Oxford English Dictionary*, January 1997, version 1.0.03 (Oxford: Oxford University Press, 1973, 1993, 1996).

7. Henry Sidgwick, *The Methods of Ethics* (Indianapolis: Hackett, 1981), 127.

8. Richard Brandt, *Ethical Theory: The Problems of Normative and Critical Ethics* (Englewood Cliffs, NJ: Prentice Hall, 1959), 306–307; Brandt, "Hedonism," 433.

9. Fred Feldman, "On the Intrinsic Value of Pleasure," *Ethics* 107 (1993): 452.

10. Ibid., 462.

11. Epicurus, "Leading Doctrines," in *Happiness: Classic and Contemporary Readings in Philosophy*, edited by Steven M. Cahn and Christine Vitrano (New York: Oxford University Press, 2008), 38.

12. Terence Irwin, *The Development of Ethics* (New York: Oxford University Press, 2007), 1:260.

13. I do not wish to imply, however, that Epicurus advocated the kind of maximizing strategy favored by Jeremy Bentham and the utilitarians. Although some theorists have argued for such an interpretation of Epicurus, I agree with Julia Annas that this is a mistake. As Annas explains, "The pleasure which we seek is not a simple feeling, as Bentham assumed. Pleasure is our final end, and as such . . . it must be something capable of organizing and focusing all the concerns and aims of my life as a whole; it must encompass everything worthwhile in my life. . . . Once pleasure is understood as it has to be in an ancient theory where it forms the agent's final end, we see that it is not the kind of thing that the agent can coherently try to maximize." Annas, *The Morality of Happiness* (New York: Oxford University Press, 1993), 85–86.

14. Epicurus, "Letter to Menoeceus," in *Happiness,* edited by Cahn and Vitrano, 36; Raymond Belliotti, *Happiness Is Overrated* (Lanham, MD: Rowman and Littlefield, 2004), 23.

15. See Richard Taylor, *Good and Evil* (Amherst, NY: Prometheus Books, 2000), 113–120. Taylor explains that for the Epicurean, "pleasure is the only ultimate good, and pain the only ultimate evil. Other things are good and bad only in relation to these. . . . Divest justice and the other commonly accepted virtues of their pleasurable fruits, and they retain nothing whatever of their goodness" (106–107).

16. Ibid., 120. See also Belliotti, who objects to Epicureanism, because "even friendship is reduced to instrumental value as its Epicurean justification is benefit to the self, not the other." Belliotti, *Happiness Is Overrated,* 27.

17. Irwin, *The Development of Ethics,* 274–275.

18. Annas, *The Morality of Happiness,* 239, 240, 341.

19. Epicurus, "Letter to Menoeceus," 35.

20. Ibid.

21. See Annas, *The Morality of Happiness,* 346; and Irwin, *The Development of Ethics,* 269.

22. A related problem is adaptation or what psychologists refer to as being on a "hedonic treadmill," which occurs when we inevitably get used to whatever pleasures we experience, leaving us craving even more. See Richard Layard, *Happiness: Lessons from a New Science* (New York: Penguin Press, 2005), 48–49.

23. Tim O'Keefe, "Epicurus," in *The Internet Encyclopedia of Philosophy,* http://www.iep.utm.edu/.

24. Epicurus, "Leading Doctrines," 36.

25. Layard, *Happiness,* 29; Gregg Easterbrook, *The Progress Paradox* (New York: Random House, 2003), xvi.

26. Easterbrook, *The Progress Paradox,* 164.

27. Epicurus, "Leading Doctrines," 39.

28. Layard, *Happiness,* 50–51.

29. Jeremy Bentham, "An Introduction to the Principles of Morals and Legislation," in *Happiness,* edited by Cahn and Vitrano, 99.

30. John Stuart Mill, "Utilitarianism," in *Happiness,* edited by Cahn and Vitrano, 122.

31. Ibid., 123.

32. Ibid., 123–124.

33. Ibid., 127.

34. Wayne Davis, "Pleasure and Happiness," *Philosophical Studies* 39 (1981): 305–317.

35. Fred Feldman, *Pleasure and the Good Life* (New York: Oxford University Press, 2006), 56.

36. Fred Feldman, *What Is This Thing Called Happiness?* (New York: Oxford University Press, 2010), 110, 137.

37. Carson, "Happiness and the Good Life," 78.

38. Daniel Haybron, "Why Hedonism Is False," in *Happiness,* edited by Cahn and Vitrano, 174.

39. L. W. Sumner, *Welfare, Happiness, and Ethics* (New York: Oxford University Press, 1996), 102.

40. Haybron, "Why Hedonism Is False," 175.

41. Ibid., 176.

42. Feldman, *What Is This Thing Called Happiness?,* 109; Feldman, *Pleasures and the Good Life,* 56.

43. Richard Taylor, *Virtue Ethics* (Amherst, NY: Prometheus Books, 2002), 109.

CHAPTER TWO

Happiness as Virtue: Plato and the Stoics

The view that happiness can be attained through a life of virtue (or moral excellence) originates with the ancient Greek and Roman ethicists, but this idea has also had a very strong influence on the way many contemporary philosophers think about happiness. Before we consider the theories themselves, we must first discuss the concept of virtue, for understanding virtue is essential for being able to critically evaluate this view of happiness. One doesn't encounter *virtue* much in everyday conversation, and I suspect the word is rarely used at all outside of philosophy classrooms. Julia Annas calls our everyday conception of virtue "unorganized" and "something of a mess," and she says our intuitions about it are "both vague and conflicting." Bernard Williams notes, "The word 'virtue' has for the most part acquired comic or otherwise undesirable associations, and few now use it except philosophers."[1]

I will confess that prior to studying philosophy, I had only the vaguest impression of what this word meant. I can recall sitting in an undergraduate ethics class where the professor asked us the simple question "What is virtue?" As my mind went completely blank, the only thought I could conjure up was that patience is a virtue, though I had no idea what that actually implied about virtue. Now, when I teach my ethics classes, I always ask my students the same question, just to see how they will respond. Usually, my question is met with several blank stares (the rest look away), and sometimes one brave soul ventures a guess that it has something to do with patience, which I suppose is something at least. But when pressed further, even the brave soul usually gives up, unable to come up with any further associations.

What I find more surprising is that vice, virtue's opposite, seems to fare no better. For instance, I often read a weekly column in the business section of the *New York Times* that features an interview with a frequent traveler. The final question they always ask the interviewee is "What is your secret airport vice?" Quite often, the replies involve things one would expect, such as eating a lot of junk food, reading tabloids, and spending too much money at airport gift shops. But there are also answers that are downright surprising, such as "I use earplugs," "I take medication to help me rest," or "I befriend the flight attendants," answers that suggest perhaps the interviewee did not quite understand the question. I have also tried asking my students about vice, thinking perhaps it was a more familiar concept that I could use to introduce virtue. But the few vague references I've gotten usually involve the seven deadly sins (of which sloth seems to be the only one anyone can remember), and I suspect the Brad Pitt movie *Seven* is the source of this weak association.

So, returning to our question, what is virtue? And why is it so vitally important to the ancient ethicists? For now, I shall provide only a sketch of virtue in broad terms, leaving the majority of the detail to be filled in by the three classic accounts we shall consider in this chapter and the next, which come from Plato, the Stoics, and Aristotle. Put simply, virtues are good character traits that people have, such as honesty, generosity, temperance, courage, and, of course, patience, which cause them to act in ways that we find admirable or praiseworthy. Annas describes virtue as "something which goes deep in the person, and is a matter of their character." Virtues involve two things that "develop together and are intertwined in practice. One is the ability to reason reflectively in the morally right way. . . . The other thing involved in virtue is a developed habit of feeling and reacting in the right way, that is, the way that accords with the correct reasoning."[2]

To fully appreciate why virtue is so important to the ancient ethicists, we must first look at what they were trying to do, for their approach to ethics is quite different from the way we conceive of morality today. What is our present conception of ethics or morality? I'm not sure that most ordinary people have a very well-developed concept of morality, especially if they have never studied philosophy in a formal setting. But I can offer some evidence based on discussions with my students. I start the first day of all ethics classes with a free association: I put up the words *ethics* and *morality* on the board, and after explaining that the two terms are generally taken to be synonymous, I ask my students what comes to mind when they see either of these terms. Usually, the first response involves some mention of "right and wrong," and that is followed up with punitive concepts such as justice, laws, rules, and punishment. Someone usually mentions religion, and sometimes there is also a reference to one's conscience and emotions such as guilt. But I almost never get any reference to the kinds of things that concerned the ancient ethicists, such as a person's character or her values; nor is there any mention of the good life, happiness, or virtue. Yet the word *ethics* actually comes from the Greek word *ethos,* meaning "character" or "custom," and the principal task of any ancient ethicist is to think about how one should live one's life, including which values and principles one should adopt. The ancient ethicists are not interested in presenting formal theories that tell us which acts are morally right or wrong; rather, they focus on questions regarding how one achieves happiness and lives a good life.

Happiness figures centrally in many ancient ethical theories, which view happiness as the final end or purpose of all human action (which they call our "telos"). Annas provides a useful description of our final end (or telos): "When we stand back a bit from our ongoing projects and ask why we are doing what we are doing, we do not find a satisfactory halt until we get to the final end which makes sense of our life as a whole."[3] For the ancient philosophers, this natural stopping point is happiness, because happiness is something that we all want, and they believe it is the pursuit of happiness that drives all of our choices. However, most people are completely ignorant about what actually causes happiness, and they spend their lives pursuing the wrong things, mistakenly believing these things will produce happiness. The ancient texts can be seen as guides or manuals offering advice on how to avoid these mistakes and live a happy life.

Although the ancient ethicists differ on the precise connection between virtue and happiness, they agree that being virtuous is a necessary component of a happy life. The importance of virtue becomes more apparent when we reflect on Aristotle's description of the virtuous person as someone who will do the right thing "at the right times, with reference to the right objects, towards the right people, with the right motive, and in the right way."[4] As this quote suggests, the basic idea is that the virtuous person is getting things right; her priorities are in good order, she makes good judgments, and she is living well overall. If we think about our lives and all of the choices we face each day, deciding what to do can be a daunting task. The virtuous person, because she has these good, stable character traits, will be able to accurately assess each situation and recognize the best way to act every time. Virtuous people also aren't prone to the rash or impulsive actions that people often regret, nor do they act out of anger or for any other shortsighted reason. The virtuous person knows what is important in her life, and she isn't swayed by short-term pleasures or temptations, because she is fully in control of her emotions. So being virtuous is not only intrinsically good (good in itself), but it is also good for you, because it promotes your well-being.

In the following sections, we shall consider two historical perspectives on how one can achieve happiness through a life of moral virtue, which come from Plato and the Stoics. We shall consider Aristotle's view of happiness in the following chapter.

Platonic Happiness

Plato (428–347 BC) is the best-known and most influential ancient Greek philosopher. Plato wrote in dialogue form, and most of his dialogues feature his teacher Socrates as the main interlocutor. In what is probably his greatest work, the *Republic,* Plato tackles the question of whether it is always better to be a just (virtuous) person rather than an unjust one.

Before we turn to Plato's actual arguments, let's first discuss what he means by justice. I've found his use of this term sometimes confuses people, for they associate justice with simply abiding by the laws or following the rules of one's society. Plato uses the term *justice* much more broadly, so that it encompasses everything we would associate with being a moral or righteous person, including all the good character traits we call virtues. So when Plato considers the question of whether justice is necessary for happiness, what he is really asking about is the connection between morality and happiness: can one be happy with a life of immorality, or is being a morally good person a necessary condition for living a happy life?

In this dialogue, Plato offers several arguments to defend the claim that being a just (morally good, virtuous) person is necessary for happiness, and his view implies the unjust (immoral, vicious) person will never be happy despite any outward appearances to the contrary. One might initially be skeptical about the connection Plato posits between virtue and happiness, because real life seems to provide so many examples of immoral people who appear to enjoy happy lives. This was my initial reaction to Plato's claim, but it is important to reserve judgment until after we have reviewed Plato's account of justice, for he does address this objection explicitly.

The *Republic* begins with Socrates posing the question "What is justice?" After several simple definitions are rejected, Socrates considers the view presented by Thrasymachus, who identifies justice as the interest of the stronger. Thrasymachus argues that the rulers of a city enact the laws that determine what is just, so we can expect these laws to promote what is in their own best interest. By following the laws of justice, we are only furthering the self-interest or happiness of the ruling class (the interest of the stronger), and this is often to our own disadvantage. Therefore, if we want to promote our own happiness, we are better off committing acts of injustice, for these will be much more profitable, assuming that we don't get caught. As Thrasymachus explains, "When a man not only seizes the property of his fellow-citizens but captures and enslaves their persons also, instead of those dishonorable titles he is called happy and highly favored, not only by the men of his own city, but also by all others who hear of the comprehensive injustice which he has wrought."[5]

Although his example may seem a bit arcane, Thrasymachus's point about the benefits of injustice should resonate, especially considering how common immorality is within our own society. Politics and business are two obvious areas in which people are frequently willing to suspend the ordinary standards of morality in order to promote their own (or their company's) interests. But even ordinary people frequently commit acts of injustice, such as driving above the speed limit, illegally downloading music from the Internet, skipping jury duty, or cheating on their taxes. Thrasymachus is arguing that we commit these acts of injustice because they make us happier than behaving justly. This is precisely the view of justice Plato wishes to refute, for he believes it is always better to be just. The challenge for Plato is to convince Thrasymachus (and us) that he is right.

In book 2 of the *Republic,* Glaucon picks up Thrasymachus's argument, challenging Socrates to convince us that "on every account it is better to be just than to be unjust."[6] Glaucon begins by distinguishing three ways in which things are good or valuable. First, we say that something has intrinsic value when we desire it solely for itself, such as feelings of enjoyment, happiness, or harmless pleasures. Second, we say that something has instrumental value when we desire that thing for its good consequences, despite the fact that it may be irksome, painful, or unpleasant. Glaucon offers exercise, undergoing medical treatments for an illness, and working to make money as examples of things with instrumental value. The final category consists of things that have both intrinsic and instrumental value, and this includes intelligence, sight, and health, because they are valued both for their own sake and for their good consequences.

Glaucon asks Socrates in which category he places justice, and Socrates replies that justice belongs in the highest category, with things valued both for their own sake and for their consequences. Glaucon replies that most people would disagree, for they view justice as belonging to the second category, with things that are "disagreeable and repulsive" in themselves but valued because of the advantages they bring.[7]

To illustrate, Glaucon relays the Myth of Gyges Ring, which is the story of a shepherd who finds a gold ring that makes its wearer invisible. Upon discovering the power of the ring, the shepherd uses it to seduce the queen, kill the king, and take possession of the throne. Glaucon has us imagine there are two rings in existence, one given to the just man and one to the unjust man, and he asks whether we expect these two men to behave any differently. Glaucon's reply is that "no one would be so steeled against temptation as to abide in the practice of justice, and resolutely to abstain from touching the property of his neighbors, when he had it in his power to help himself without fear to anything he pleased in the market, or to go into private houses and have intercourse with whom he would, or to kill and release from prison according to his own pleasure, and in everything else to act among men with the power of a god."[8]

Glaucon is arguing that the just man would behave no differently from the unjust man, for both would be tempted to satisfy their own desires. Furthermore, we recognize committing injustice as a rational choice, especially if it is unlikely one will be caught. Glaucon even argues, "If anyone having this license [possession of the ring] within his grasp were to refuse to do any injustice, or to touch the property of others, all who were aware of it would think him a most pitiful and irrational creature."[9] He concludes that justice is only instrumentally valuable; we behave justly because we lack the power to commit acts of injustice with impunity, and we are afraid of the consequences. But justice (in itself) has no special value, for when the fear of punishment is removed, no sane person would continue to behave justly.

As a final illustration of his argument, Glaucon asks us to compare the lives of two people, one who is perfectly just and the other perfectly unjust, to see who is actually better off. The perfectly unjust man, we are told, is morally depraved and vicious, but he maintains the appearance of justice. Because he is *perfectly* unjust, he has everyone fooled into thinking he is the most honorable and respected member of society. He is loved by all, and he enjoys a life blessed with money and privilege, powerful friends, a wonderful wife, and successful children. In contrast, the perfectly just man is stripped of everything but his justice. Although he is truly noble and good, he enjoys none of the benefits of justice, because his society thinks he is a scoundrel. Given his terrible reputation, Glaucon tells us, the perfectly just man will be "scourged, racked, fettered, will have his eyes burnt out, and at last, after suffering every kind of torture, will be crucified."[10] The simple question is: which man is better off? This example is especially challenging for Plato, because his view of justice implies the perfectly just man must be happier than the perfectly unjust man, when just the opposite seems to be true.

To answer this challenge, Plato appeals to the effect of justice (or morally good behavior) on the state of a person's soul. Plato begins with a description of the soul as consisting of three distinct parts, which one can think of as three distinct and competing motivations. Although the terminology Plato uses to describe our psychology may sound a bit archaic (today, we are probably more likely to refer to a person's "mind" or "consciousness" rather than her "soul"), his description of how our motivations can compete against each other for primacy actually makes a lot of intuitive sense. Consider an example. You are stuck in traffic, and there appears to be a bad accident up ahead with several dead bodies strewn among the wreckage. As you approach the accident, part of you wants to slow down and look. But at the same time, part of you does not want to witness the gruesome scene, which you will probably find disturbing.

You may struggle with yourself, turning your head away as you get close, but the urge to look just as you are in front of the accident may overwhelm you. Plato describes the competing pull of these two opposing motivations as taking place between two different parts of your soul.

According to Plato, altogether, there are three distinct parts of the soul, which he refers to as reason, spirit, and appetite. Reason is the rational part whose job it is to exercise forethought on behalf of the whole person and to make wise decisions. Reason can be compared to the little angel sitting on our shoulder urging us to get to work on time, quit smoking, and eat more vegetables. Spirit is the emotional part, which is naturally allied with reason, and spirit helps us to act on reason's commands. Appetite is the irrational part, which impels us to indulge in pleasures. Appetite is like the little devil sitting on the other shoulder, the one who tempts us to eat another piece of chocolate cake or to go out drinking even though we know we have to get up early the next morning. Plato warns that appetite must be controlled by reason and spirit, because it is the largest part of the soul, and it will get out of hand if it is overindulged.

According to Plato, a person has a just soul when all three parts are working in unison to promote the well-being or good of the person, with each part doing its own proper work. Reason issues commands about what is in the individual's best interest, and spirit is working together with reason to tame the appetite. Because her soul is in balance, the just person will experience a kind of psychic harmony and inner peace. Put simply, she will be happy.

Plato describes the person whose soul is in balance as entirely virtuous, for she will embody each of the four cardinal virtues: wisdom, courage, temperance (or moderation), and justice. She will be wise, because reason is providing guidance about what is best for her. She will be courageous, because her spirited part is listening to reason about which situations she should fear, and she won't be swayed by the momentary pains or pleasures that cause people to act in cowardly or rash ways. She will be temperate (or moderate), because her appetite is controlled by spirit and reason, and all three parts are in agreement. Finally, she will be just, because justice is defined as having an ordered soul with all three parts functioning well together. Within the just person, every part does its proper job, and none exerts more authority than it should. Plato describes the just person as having achieved self-mastery; she does not experience any of the inner turmoil that leads to unhappiness. Therefore, on Plato's view, the just person is happy, because she has a healthy, well-balanced soul.

Alternatively, acts of injustice cause strife among the parts of the soul. Because the unjust person's soul is out of balance, the three parts will meddle and interfere with each other, not listening to reason. The unjust person may become self-indulgent, and she will be tempted to pursue harmful pleasures. Once the soul is imbalanced, there will be confusion among the parts of the soul, and this person will suffer from tremendous inner turmoil. The unjust person will experience intense urges for the wrong things, feeling constantly outmatched and overwhelmed by her desires. Even if she is able to fulfill some of her desires, she will never feel satisfied or content, because her appetite will always be raging.

Plato believed that every just (or morally good) act serves to reinforce the inner harmony within our souls, and he describes the just soul as healthy, beautiful, and in accord with nature. Alternatively, acts of injustice lead to disorder among the parts, and Plato describes the unjust person as having a disease that violates our true nature. Therefore, Plato's reply to Glaucon's challenge is quite clear: acts of justice will always make us happier than acts of injustice, because only justice will preserve the harmony within our souls. One should never be tempted to commit unjust or immoral acts, because they will make the soul sick by encouraging discord among the parts. Whatever reward one hopes to reap from such unjust behavior, such as money or power, it will be useless if one's soul is corrupted and ruined. Therefore, Plato believes that justice is necessary for living a happy life, because it promotes order within the soul.

Jeffrie Murphy is a contemporary philosopher who agrees with Plato about the necessary connection between happiness and moral behavior. Murphy argues that the whole point of philosophizing about happiness is to supply this notion with content. Although the uneducated masses might consider someone like the perfectly unjust man to be happy, because they associate happiness with earthly possessions and power, the philosopher can provide a more enlightened understanding of happiness that shows why he is not really happy. Murphy argues that Plato is trying to advance our philosophical understanding of happiness by suggesting that "full human happiness is to be understood as the satisfaction one takes in having a personality wherein all the elements required for a fully realized human life are harmoniously integrated."[11]

Philippa Foot advocates a similar view of happiness, for she argues that "great happiness, unlike euphoria or even great pleasure, must come from something related to what is deep in human nature, and fundamental in human life, such as affection for children and friends, the desire to work, and love of freedom and truth." Since the unjust person lacks many of these attributes, including integrity, moral emotions, and the capacity for true friendships, it follows that she cannot really be happy in the full sense used by philosophers. Murphy believes the unjust person is probably afraid of having her true nature revealed, and that fear is also incompatible with genuine happiness. Murphy concludes that when he thinks of someone like the perfectly unjust man, he pities this person, because "he is punished simply by being the kind of person he is. But why would I pity him if I thought he was truly happy?"[12]

Plato's view of happiness, which is endorsed by Murphy and Foot, implies the immoralist, or the person who knowingly commits acts of injustice, can never be happy, because her soul is sick. When we think about some of the reasons people give to explain their bad behavior, Plato's description of the disordered soul is especially accurate. For example, crimes of passion, cases of road rage, and brawls in bars often involve people getting carried away by their irrational side, following their raging appetites instead of listening to reason. In other cases, highly intelligent and accomplished people get overwhelmed by a traumatic life event, which causes them to act in highly irrational and often immoral ways. For example, Lisa Nowak was a married mother of three children and a NASA astronaut when a breakup with her lover caused her to drive nine hundred miles (wearing a diaper, so she would not have to stop) in order to confront her romantic rival. She has since been arrested and charged with attempted murder and kidnapping. More recently, Amy Bishop, a University of Alabama biology professor, shot six faculty members at a department meeting shortly after being denied tenure.

Plato's picture of the disordered soul provides a good explanation of the psychology of people who act in rash, impulsive, and obviously regrettable ways, people whose behavior is not just immoral but also irrational. One wants to ask the people in these examples, what on earth were you thinking? What could you possibly have hoped to gain by acting in this way? On Plato's view, the answer is simple: they were not thinking clearly, because reason was not in control of the nonrational parts of their soul, appetite, and spirit. These cases demonstrate how committing acts of injustice can lead to unhappiness, and they suggest that if you are interested in promoting your own happiness, you have a serious reason to refrain from immoral behavior, which might disturb the balance within your soul.

But now we must ask how well Plato's analysis describes the case of the perfectly unjust man described by Glaucon. Plato must say the perfectly unjust man's happiness is merely an illusion, because his acts of injustice imply that he has a disordered soul. Although this analysis may sound comforting, for no one wants to see the "bad guy" flourish, one might not find it entirely convincing. Consider all of the cases within business and politics where people commit white-collar crimes. These immoral and blatantly unjust acts often lack the impulsive, emotional, irrational characteristics that one would expect from a person who is dominated by one of the nonrational parts of the soul. Rather, these cunning immoralists appear to be in complete control of their emotions, and their immoral behavior often results in their getting exactly what they want. Plato's model seems to assimilate all wrongdoing to the work of a raging appetite and spirit that dominate or overpower reason. One might wonder whether Plato's model actually captures the thriving immoralist Glaucon portrays, the person who is such a good actor that he has everyone fooled. The perfectly unjust man does not appear to be controlled by a raging appetite, and his ability to keep his immorality concealed suggests reason is more in control than Plato would like to admit. It is comforting to think that, eventually, even the perfectly unjust man will get caught (like Bernie Madoff). But until that day comes, one might wonder how Plato can deny the perfectly unjust man's happiness. The problem is that certain criminals seem to exhibit excellent self-control and very good instrumental reasoning, and their immoral behavior does not seem "crazy" or blatantly self-destructive. On the contrary, they often appear to enjoy the kind of psychic harmony Plato associates with having a just soul (at least until they get caught).

David Sachs raises a related concern about Plato's conception of justice. Sachs argues that "Plato thought that men who were just according to his conception of justice would pass the tests of ordinary morality. But although Plato more than once has Socrates say things to this effect, he nowhere tries to prove it. Attempts to show that Platonic justice entails ordinary morality are strikingly missing from the *Republic;* Plato merely assumes that having the one involves having the other."[13]

The problem, according to Sachs, is that the virtues exhibited by a just soul, such as wisdom, courage, and temperance, are entirely compatible with "a variety of vulgar injustices and evil-doing. Neither as usually understood nor as Plato characterizes them are those virtues inconsistent with performing any of the acts Thrasymachus and Glaucon mention as examples of injustice. In this regard, it is tempting to assert that the most that can be said on behalf of Plato's argument is that crimes and evils could not be done by a Platonically just man in a foolish, unintelligent, cowardly or uncontrolled way." Sachs concludes that "neither separately nor conjointly do the theses of Books VIII and IX [Plato's *Republic*] . . . exclude the possibility of men whose souls are Platonically just committing what would ordinarily be judged immoral acts."[14]

Sachs's argument calls into question Plato's analysis of the perfectly unjust man, for it implies that having a just soul is no guarantee that one will behave morally. The perfectly unjust man described by Glaucon is someone who reasons well about how to satisfy his desires and fools everyone about the deviant nature of his character. Sachs's argument suggests it is possible the perfectly unjust man has a just soul (with reason dominating the two nonrational parts), and this would explain how he is such a successful immoralist. But if the perfectly unjust man has a just soul, then according to Plato's own reasoning, he is also happy.

Raymond Belliotti also questions whether Plato proves the unjust person is always doomed to unhappiness. Belliotti explains that according to Plato, "The unjust soul is unhealthy due to internal disharmony. Unjust people are not happy regardless of external appearances that suggest otherwise. In the same way that physically unhealthy people may seem healthy to their acquaintances, unhealthy souls cannot always be detected by the naked eye. Injustice, nevertheless, manifests an illness that is never in the interests of the perpetrator." Belliotti agrees with Plato when we are assessing "a thoroughly and morally depraved, intellectually bankrupt tyrant. Most such people are unlikely to be happy. Their excesses are themselves often attributable to their unhappiness and inability to adapt to their social environments. Even their episodic satisfactions evaporate quickly." However, Belliotti finds Plato's argument much less convincing "if we are assessing the vast majority of human beings who are neither moral paragons nor unrepentant tyrants. That people can be reasonably happy while falling far short of being moral and intellectual paragons remains plausible. Consult your own lives and those of your peers."[15]

Before we reject Plato's analysis of the perfectly unjust man, however, we must consider what Plato (and his defenders) might say in response to these objections. First, it should be emphasized that Plato does address the cunning criminal who carefully plans his acts of immorality and avoids detection. Plato offers several specific examples of deviant people (which he refers to as timocratic, oligarchic, and democratic) who "have rational plans for their lives and execute them steadily, without especially frequent lapses into incontinence," or a lack of self-control. As Terence Irwin explains:

> The timocratic person need not be specially prone to imprudent bursts of anger; indeed, his plans encourage him to control his appetites and emotions in order to pursue his long-term aim of honour and reputation more efficiently. The single-minded and systematic planning of the oligarchic person is strongly emphasized. . . . The democratic person acts on a variety of desires with no clear hierarchical structure, but this is not because he cannot control his desires. On the contrary, his rational plan is precisely to leave his different desires a certain agree of freedom, and in acting on them he does just what he rationally plans to do.[16]

Therefore, Plato was clearly aware of the existence of the cunning criminal, whose acts of immorality are not rash, irrational, or blatantly self-destructive.

Plato would certainly object to calling the cunning criminal just, even though she exhibits good instrumental reasoning about how to satisfy her desires, for Plato would also take into account the nature of a person's desires. Irwin suggests that a soul dominated by reason has "formed desires resting on wise deliberation about what is good for the whole soul and it uses these desires to guide the whole soul."[17] Plato would argue that the immoralist's desires are defective, because they do not reflect what is good for her as a person. Immoral desires originate not from reason, but from one of the two nonrational parts of the soul, whose view of what is good is naturally limited.

As Irwin explains, the rational part "incorporates, but also modifies, the outlooks of the two non-rational parts. If we can see all four sides of a building, we can understand the points of view of four observers each of whom can observe only one side; each point of view is misleading by itself, and even the sum of their four points of view is misleading, but we can see how far they are accurate if we understand the whole building of which they observe different parts. The rational part takes this wider point of view on the desires and interests of the non-rational parts, so that it can satisfy their interests better than it would if it simply chose to be guided by their desires."[18]

Acting on desires that reflect a person's entire good is important, because whenever we act on our desires, we have certain expectations about the satisfaction we will experience. Under the best circumstances, our expectations will accurately represent how we will feel after we get what we want. Suppose I have always wanted to be a famous actress, because I love being the center of attention. If my expectations about what being famous is like are accurate, I stand a good chance of being happy once I achieve my goal. But if my expectations are wildly mistaken, I may get exactly what I want, yet be miserable. When we are dominated by the nonrational parts of our souls, we are being led by our desires for various things, but the nonrational parts lack the perspective to accurately gauge whether these desires will actually make us happy. Satisfying desires formed by the nonrational parts could be deeply disappointing, unsatisfying, or harmful, because these desires may not reflect what is good for the person as a whole. As Irwin explains:

> Since the non-rational parts are moved by present inclination when they form their aims, they are easily misled by misleading features of the background that forms their present inclination. The rational part, by contrast, is concerned to find what is really better and worse on the whole. This concern with truth leads it to pursue the true good of the whole soul. If it takes this point of view, it does not form its aims simply on the basis of the strength of its inclinations, and so it will not make its choices in the distorting conditions that influence the non-rational parts.[19]

I leave it to the reader to decide who makes the better case—Plato or Glaucon—regarding the perfectly unjust man's happiness. Whereas some theorists have found Plato's analysis less than convincing, perhaps most notably Aristotle, as we shall see in the next chapter, Plato has certainly anticipated these kinds of objections and does offer a reply to them. We shall return to the question of whether virtue is actually necessary for happiness in the final section of the next chapter, where I shall critically evaluate this view. First, we must consider another historical perspective on the connection between virtue and happiness.

Stoic Happiness

Stoicism was founded by Zeno (344–262 BC) during the Hellenistic period, though only fragments of his work or those of his immediate predecessors survive. The complete works we do have by Stoic philosophers come from Seneca (4 BC–AD 65), Epictetus (AD 55–135), and the emperor Marcus Aurelius (AD 121–180). Stoicism was initially popular within ancient Greece, but it spread to the Roman Empire, where it appealed to the Roman character as "a code which was manly, rational and temperate, a code which insisted on just and virtuous dealing, self-discipline, unflinching fortitude, and complete freedom from the storms of passion."[20]

Like Plato and many other ancient moralists, the Stoics begin from a reflection on the agent's final good (or telos), which they equate with happiness. Seneca explains, "To live happily . . . is the desire of all men, but their minds are blinded to a clear vision of just what it is that makes life happy; and so far from its being easy to attain the happy life, the more eagerly a man strives to reach it, the farther he recedes from it if he has made the mistake in the road; for when it leads in the opposite direction, his very speed will increase the distance that separates him." The Stoics agree with Plato that virtue is a necessary component of the happy life, but they believe happiness is attained by "living in accord with nature," and they associate virtue with using reason to control your will. The early Stoic Arius Didymus explains, "One's aim, they say, is being happy, for the sake of which everything is done, while it is not done for the sake of anything further; and this consists in living according to virtue, in living in agreement and further (it is the same thing) in living according to nature."[21]

Before we go further, we should get clear on what the Stoics mean by nature, for they aren't suggesting that we take up organic farming or join a hippie commune. Rather, they are referring to the nature of the universe, or "cosmic nature," which they believe exhibits rational planning and order. The Stoics are causal determinists, meaning they believe every event that occurs in the present was caused by some prior event in the past, and this chain of events goes all the way back to the beginning of time. Put simply, the determinist would say that whatever is happening right now is inevitable or predetermined given what has happened before it. Since every event within the universe contributes to its ultimate perfection, everything that happens in nature is for the best, even if we, as human beings, cannot appreciate that from our limited perspective.

In a humorous example that illustrates how the Stoics view every natural occurrence as having an important purpose, Annas cites Plutarch as saying that mice encourage us to be careful not to leave things lying around, while bedbugs help us to get up in the morning and be productive. To use another example, human beings often attach emotional significance to natural events, such as hurricanes, floods, and fires, viewing them as awful or devastating, because they cause damage to our property and homes. But the Stoics would argue that these natural occurrences should not provoke an emotional reaction at all, because they are simply a necessary part of the natural world. Although we might be tempted to make negative judgments concerning them, the Stoic would advise us to view everything that is beyond our control with complete emotional detachment or indifference. As Marcus Aurelius succinctly explains, "Put from you the belief that 'I have been wronged,' and with it will go the feeling. Reject your sense of injury, and the injury itself disappears."[22]

The Stoics believe the entire natural world is pursuing its final purpose and that human beings are just one small part of that world. Marcus Aurelius explains, "Universal Nature's impulse was to create an orderly world. It follows, then, that everything now happening must follow a logical sequence. . . . Remembrance of this will help you face many things more calmly." As human beings, we can achieve virtue by using reason to understand nature. Essential to this understanding is grasping the distinction between what we can control and what we cannot and concerning ourselves only with what is within our control. All natural occurrences are inevitable or predetermined, so they are beyond our control; our judgments or reactions to those occurrences, however, are within our control. When natural events occur, the Stoic maintains the proper attitude of "apathy" or emotional indifference to them. Marcus Aurelius explains how one achieves this apathetic attitude: "Think of the totality of all Being, and what a mite of it is yours; think of all Time, and the brief fleeting instant of it that is allotted to yourself; think of Destiny, and how puny a part of it you are."[23]

Annas explains that the Stoics who are virtuous will exhibit a complete lack of feeling or emotion, because "they stress the importance of the cognitive side of virtue, regarding it in very intellectual ways, and say roundly that there is

no degree of feeling that it is appropriate for the virtuous person to have."
The Stoic philosopher Arius further explains their view of the emotions: "A
feeling . . . is an impulse which is excessive and disobedient to reason . . . or,
an <irrational> movement in the soul contrary to nature. . . . And 'contrary
to nature' is understood in the sketch of feeling as something happening contrary to the reason which is correct and according to nature."[24]

Therefore, the Stoics associate virtue with eliminating all emotion, because they view the emotions as contrary to reason, and, therefore, contrary
to nature.[25] The Stoics believe the virtuous person will choose to do the right
thing, simply because she recognizes (through the use of reason) that it is
the right thing to do, and not because she feels an emotional impulse, which
is unreliable. By severing the connection between morality and emotion, the
Stoics make it possible for anyone to develop a virtuous character, because
virtue depends solely on reason and the power of your own will. It is essential
to the Stoic conception of virtue that you remain unemotional or indifferent
to whatever happens by chance, not allowing any external events to disturb
you. Consider the following passage from Marcus Aurelius, who encourages
us to focus on the things we can control, such as the development of our
characters:

> You will never be remarkable for quick-wittedness. Be it so, then; yet there are
> still a host of other qualities whereof you cannot say, "I have no bent for them."
> Cultivate these, then, for they are wholly within your power: sincerity, for ex-
> ample, and dignity; industriousness, and sobriety. Avoid grumbling; be frugal,
> considerate, and frank; be temperate in manner and in speech; carry yourself
> with authority. See how many qualities there are which could be yours at this
> moment. You can allege no naïve incapacity or inaptitude for them; and yet you
> choose to linger still on a less lofty plane. Furthermore, is it any lack of natural
> endowments that necessitate those fits of querulousness and parsimony and ful-
> some flattery, of railing at your ill-health, of cringing and bragging and contin-
> ually veering from one mood to another? Most assuredly not; you could have
> rid yourself of all these long ago, and remained chargeable with nothing worse
> than a certain slowness and dullness of comprehension—and even this you can
> correct with practice, so long as you do not make light of it or take pleasure in
> your own obtuseness.[26]

The Stoics believe there is no good or evil in the world, for all good and evil consists in our own minds and judgments. Since we have control over our own minds, it follows that nothing that happens in the world can affect us unless we allow it to. According to the Stoics, all of the unhappiness we experience is caused by our judgment that certain events are bad or harmful. But these events are external to us, and since they are beyond our control, we should not let them affect our happiness.

There is some truth to what the Stoics say about happiness, because people often become unhappy when they start making demands on the universe and the universe fails to deliver. The Stoics would say the problem is not with the universe or the natural order of things; the problem is with us, or rather with our judgments. As Epictetus explains:

> What disturbs men's mind is not events but judgments on events. For instance, death is nothing dreadful, or else Socrates would have thought so. No, the only dreadful thing about it is men's judgment that it is dreadful. And so when we are hindered, or disturbed, or distressed, let us never lay the blame on others, but on ourselves, that is, on our own judgments. To accuse others for one's own misfortunes is a sign of want of education; to accuse oneself shows that one's education has begun; to accuse neither oneself nor others shows that one's education is complete.[27]

Consider an example. You are waiting for the bus on a cold, windy day, and it has just started to rain. You are becoming increasingly uncomfortable as the wind blows the rain underneath your flimsy umbrella, and you can feel the water starting to soak through your clothes and shoes. As you realize the bus is delayed, your anger and unhappiness intensify, so that now, in addition to being cold and wet, you are also quite miserable. However, the bus delay and dreadful weather conditions are completely beyond your control. By letting these external events negatively affect your mood, the Stoics would argue, you are ultimately responsible for your own unhappiness. The ideal Stoic sage will acknowledge that she is cold and wet, but she will refuse to let these sensations bother her. Instead, she will view the weather and the delay with apathy or indifference, thereby maintaining her happiness. As Epictetus explains, "Make it your study then to confront every harsh impression with the words, 'You are but an impression and not at all what you seem to be.' Then test it by those rules that you possess; and first by this—chief test of all—'Is it concerned with what is in our power or with what is not in our power?' And if it is concerned with what is not in our power, be ready with the answer that it is nothing to you."[28]

Therefore, the Stoic experiences all of the same sensations, pleasures, and pains as everyone else; the difference lies in her reaction to them, for she experiences them as things that do not matter. Epictetus explains:

> It is silly to want your children and your wife and your friends to live forever, for that means that you want what is not in your control to be in your control, and what is not your own to be yours. . . . Exercise yourself then in what lies in your power. Each man's master is the man who has authority over what he wishes or does not wish, to secure the one or to take away the other. Let him then who wishes to be free not wish for anything or avoid anything that depends on others; or else he is bound to be a slave.[29]

There are several similarities between the Stoics and Plato, for both believe that virtue is necessary for achieving happiness, and both identify the virtuous person as having reason firmly in control of her emotions and appetite (or the will). Both views imply that what matters for happiness is not what happens in the external world, but what happens within your own mind or soul, and both associate the happy life with maintaining inner harmony or tranquillity. The Stoics would have no problem accepting the happiness of Plato's just man on the rack, for they would not view his external suffering as an adversity that should diminish his happiness. As Epictetus explains, "Sickness is a hindrance to the body, but not to the will, unless the will consent. Lameness is a hindrance to the leg, but not to the will. Say this to yourself at each event that happens, for you shall find that though it hinders something else it will not hinder you."[30]

Another similarity between Plato and the Stoics is the role reason plays in their ethical systems. For Plato, reason acts as a commander who uses spirit to control the appetite. As long as reason dominates the soul, Plato believes, we have what is necessary for achieving happiness. The Stoics offer a similar picture, for although they do not emphasize controlling our desires, they focus on achieving a state of detachment, such that we remain perfectly content regardless of what happens in the external world. Both strategies seek to protect us from the kinds of dissatisfaction that often lead to unhappiness.

Although the Stoic strategy of remaining indifferent to devastating adversities is admirable, I wonder whether exerting such fierce control over our emotions does not also inhibit or limit the experience of happiness. Some theorists, most notably Aristotle, deem the emotions an essential part of living a happy life. Trying to eliminate the emotions you feel may help to blunt the traumas you experience in life, but it is doubtful whether these strategies will do much to promote your happiness, especially when you consider how much a person's happiness is connected with loving others and being attached to people. If you are a good Stoic, you will not let yourself be consumed by any emotions, but that strategy may also preclude being deeply involved with other people.

Raymond Belliotti raises a related concern about the implications of Stoicism: "Grieving, sorrow, and suffering are not inherently evil. Human beings are by nature valuing creatures. We cannot be stonily indifferent and retain our humanity. To value something is to make it an object of concern. . . . If we remain indifferent to the loss of what we value we call into question the intensity of our commitment. . . . Because our evaluations, convictions, and actions define our lives, we cannot be indifferent to our defeats, disappointments, and losses. . . . We should not cry over spilled milk. We should cry over spilled blood."[31]

Richard Taylor offers the following description of a good Stoic, which further emphasizes this objection: "You *act* as you would act if you loved, but you resolutely suppress any inclination to love, for that is a mere feeling and hence irrational. The compelling force for the Stoic in such a situation is not one's obligations *to others,* much less any love for them, but rather, one's obligation *to oneself.* That obligation is, as always, to tend and reinforce one's own excellence as a person. . . . You help the suffering, not for their sake, but because to do otherwise would be to compromise the sense of obligation that is essential to a truly noble life."[32]

Consider the following passages from Epictetus: "Remember always to say to yourself, 'What is its nature?' If you are fond of a jug, say you are fond of a jug; then you will not be disturbed if it be broken. If you kiss your child or your wife, say to yourself that you are kissing a human being, for then if death strikes it you will not be disturbed." Epictetus also advises, "Never say of anything, 'I lost it', but say, 'I gave it back.' Has your child died? It was given back. Has your wife died? She was given back. Has your estate been taken from you? Was not this also given back? But you say, 'He who took it from me is wicked.' What does it matter to you through whom the Giver asked it back? As long as He gives it to you, take care of it, but not as your own; treat it as passers-by treat an inn."[33]

The problem with Stoicism is that it encourages emotional detachment, but one might worry that this also includes distancing oneself from other people.[34] By keeping ourselves apathetic or indifferent to what happens to other people, as Epictetus advises, it seems we are missing out on one of the greatest sources of joy available to human beings. Being apathetic will certainly protect us from experiencing pain, but it may also prohibit us from experiencing the full range of human happiness. Therefore, maintaining an attitude of Stoic indifference does not appear to be a realistic way of achieving happiness for most ordinary people, for there is an important difference between a life that contains no emotional pain or suffering and one that is genuinely happy. Although I believe we can all benefit from adopting the Stoic's attitude of indifference when we find ourselves facing adversities, I am not convinced it is the best strategy for living a happy life. Achieving happiness seems to require more than simply avoiding unhappiness.

In response, the defender of Stoicism could argue that we have misunderstood Epictetus, who did not advocate adopting a careless attitude toward our loved ones. As Irwin explains:

> [Epictetus] does not imply that the death of a child or friend really matters no more than the breaking of a pot. He advises us to use this thought to dislodge us from our previous attachment to external goods. He assumes that we need to counter a tendency in our appearances to go too far, and that we can do this by taking account of features of the situation that a particular appearance tends to neglect. The appearances that underlie passions tend to draw our attention to only one of the practically relevant aspects of a situation. Sometimes they draw our attention to the most relevant feature, but sometimes they mislead us by diverting attention from equally relevant or more relevant features. Epictetus wants us to recall features that we tend to overlook because of the appearance that underlies the passion. The comparison between the loss of a child and the loss of a cup reminds us of our conviction that good and ill fortune are no part of happiness, since they are no part of virtue. If we keep this in mind, we will not confuse cases in which we lose a preferred indifferent [someone we care about] with cases in which life is not worth living because we are really deprived of happiness.[35]

William Irvine argues that the Stoic technique of "negative visualization" (which involves our contemplation of the bad things that can happen to us) may cause us to value those things more. For example, by contemplating the death of our relatives and friends, "we will be less likely to take our friends for granted, and as a result, we will probably derive far more pleasure from friendships than we otherwise would."[36]

The Stoic's view of emotions is also a source of debate among scholars. For instance, Michael Frede argues that the Stoics do not advocate eliminating *all* emotions, but only those that are irrational. "The rational emotions are those of a perfectly rational reason whose sentiments are not coloured and intensified or weakened by any false assumptions, assumptions, e.g. concerning the value of the things we are attracted or repelled by." Therefore, it is a mistake to assume the Stoic sage does not experience any feelings or have any human concerns. Rather, "things do move him, but not in such a way as to disturb his balanced judgment and make him attribute an importance to them which they do not have." Terence Irwin agrees with this interpretation, for he says that the Stoic has "good affections" that "allow him joy, caution, and wish. . . . The good affective states are reasonable reactions to situations that provoke passions in other people."[37]

Given the disagreements among scholars over how to interpret the Stoics, it is difficult to issue a judgment regarding the success of their strategies for achieving happiness. Thankfully, we need not settle this debate in order to evaluate the question of whether virtue is necessary for happiness. However, before turning to that question, we must first consider one more classic view, a view that has probably exerted the most influence in shaping the way contemporary theorists view happiness. We shall begin the next chapter by discussing Aristotle's view of happiness, and then we can critically evaluate the claim that virtue is necessary for achieving happiness.

Notes

1. Julia Annas, "Virtue and Eudaimonism," in *Happiness: Classic and Contemporary Readings in Philosophy,* edited by Steven M. Cahn and Christine Vitrano (New York: Oxford University Press, 2008), 246; Julia Annas, *The Morality of Happiness* (New York: Oxford University Press, 1993), 5.

2. Annas, "Virtue and Eudaimonism," 247–248.

3. Annas, *The Morality of Happiness,* 43.

4. Aristotle, *Nicomachean Ethics,* in *Happiness,* edited by Cahn and Vitrano, 26.

5. Plato, *Republic,* in *Ethics: History, Theory, and Contemporary Issues,* edited by Steven M. Cahn and Peter Markie (New York: Oxford University Press, 2006), 57.

6. Ibid., 65.

7. Ibid.

8. Ibid., 67.

9. Ibid.

10. Ibid., 68.

11. Jeffrie Murphy, "Happiness and Immorality," in *Happiness,* edited by Cahn and Vitrano, 263.

12. Philippa Foot, *Moral Dilemmas* (Oxford: Clarendon Press, 2002), 35; Murphy, "Happiness and Immorality," 264.

13. David Sachs, "A Fallacy in Plato's *Republic,*" in *Plato: A Collection of Critical Essays,* edited by Gregory Vlastos (Garden City, NY: Anchor Books, 1971), 48.

14. Ibid.

15. Raymond Belliotti, *Happiness Is Overrated* (Lanham, MD: Rowman and Littlefield, 2004), 9–10.

16. Terence Irwin, *Plato's Ethics* (New York: Oxford University Press, 1995), 284.

17. Terence Irwin, *The Development of Ethics* (Oxford: Oxford University Press, 2007), 1:103.

18. Ibid.

19. Irwin, *Plato's Ethics,* 293–294.

20. Marcus Aurelius, *Mediations,* translated by Maxwell Staniforth (New York: Penguin Books, 1964), 10.

21. Seneca, "On the Happy Life," in *Happiness,* edited by Cahn and Vitrano, 41; Annas, *The Morality of Happiness,* 163.

22. Annas, *The Morality of Happiness,* 161; Aurelius, *Mediations,* 65.

23. Ibid., 19, 86.

24. Annas, *The Morality of Happiness,* 61, 62.

25. However, some commentators believe the Stoics did not advocate the elimination of *all* emotions, but only the negative ones. For instance, in *A Guide to the Good Life* (Oxford: Oxford University Press, 2009), William Irvine argues that contrary to popular assumption, the Stoics valued joy and "the phrase 'joyful Stoic' is not an oxymoron" (48). "Rather than being passive individuals who were grimly resigned to being on the receiving end of the world's abuse and injustice, the Stoics were fully engaged in life and worked hard to make the world a better place" (8).

26. Aurelius, *Mediations,* 78–79.

27. Epictetus, "Enchiridion," in *Ethics,* edited by Cahn and Markie, 184–185.

28. Ibid., 184.

29. Ibid., 186.

30. Ibid., 185.

31. Belliotti, *Happiness Is Overrated,* 31.

32. Richard Taylor, *Virtue Ethics* (Amherst, NY: Prometheus Books, 2002), 50.

33. Epictetus, "Enchiridion," 184, 185.

34. The Stoics did believe in the process of social *oikeiosis* (familiarity), which Annas describes as resulting in an extension of "our other-concern in a steadily more rational way until we come to have the same degree of rational other-concern for all other rational beings" (*The Morality of Happiness,* 302). But the goal of this process is increasing impartiality; we extend our moral concern for others outward to include not just our immediate friends and family but more distant relatives and eventually strangers. Although this process of *oikeiosis* implies that we have connections with other people, its emphasis on impartiality invites additional objections. As Annas notes, "Impartiality has seemed to many to be too high a demand for a reasonable morality to make, too much of an alienation from our natural attachments to be a requirement that moral agents can reasonably be expected to respect" (267).

35. Irwin, *The Development of Ethics,* 345.

36. Irvine, *Guide to the Good Life,* 70.

37. Michael Frede, "The Stoic Doctrine of the Affections of the Soul," in *The Norms of Nature,* edited by Malcolm Schofield and Gisela Striker (Cambridge: Cambridge University Press, 1986), 94, 110; Irwin, *The Development of Ethics,* 343.

CHAPTER THREE

Happiness as Virtue: Aristotle

Aristotle begins *Nicomachean Ethics* with this statement: "Every art and every inquiry, and similarly every action and pursuit, is thought to aim at some good."[1] Aristotle's statement is a simple truism: whenever anyone acts, we assume she is motivated by something she sees as good. Some goods, Aristotle tells us, are subordinate to others. For instance, exercise is a subordinate good, because we exercise in order to achieve physical fitness and health. But the highest good (our "telos") is not subordinate to anything, for it is something we desire intrinsically or solely for its own sake. Following Plato and the Stoics, whose views we considered in the previous chapter, Aristotle identifies the highest good with happiness.[2] He explains, "Verbally, there is very general agreement [as to the highest of all goods achievable by action] for both the general run of men and people of superior refinement say that it is happiness, and identify living well and doing well with being happy; but with regard to what happiness is they differ, and many do not give the same account as the wise."[3]

Aristotle offers an argument to support his identification of happiness with the highest good. He tells us the highest human good must meet the following two criteria: it is complete, meaning it is desirable solely for its own sake, and it is self-sufficient, meaning it lacks nothing. Among the suggestions he considers for what might be the highest good, including wealth, honor, and pleasure, only happiness meets both of these criteria. Therefore, happiness must be the highest good.

Aristotle's conclusion that happiness meets both criteria is supported by reflecting on our ordinary attitudes about happiness. Regarding the first criterion, it does seem wrong to say that someone could be seeking happiness instrumentally; it is difficult to understand how someone could want happiness for any reason other than its own intrinsic properties. Furthermore, happiness, when offered as an explanation for action, puts an end to all chains of reasoning: if someone explains why she is doing something by saying, "Because it will make me happy," no further reasons are necessary. Happiness is self-sufficient, because it encompasses all the other goals a person might have. For instance, you work in order to make money, which in turn makes you feel secure and gives you a sense of pride and accomplishment. But all of these goals are part of the highest good, which is happiness.

Aristotle's argument only establishes that happiness is the highest or chief good; it does not provide much content to the notion of happiness. Aristotle acknowledges this and explains, "Presumably, however, to say that happiness is the chief good seems a platitude, and a clearer account of what it is is still desired. This might perhaps be given, if we could first ascertain the function of man . . . for all things that have a function or activity, the good and the 'well' is thought to reside in the function, so would it seem to be for man, if he has a function."[4]

Aristotle is suggesting "the good" of anything that has a function is going to be directly related to that function. For example, we say a water bottle is good when it performs the function of water bottles well. Applying this reasoning to human beings, who also have a distinct function, we could say that someone is living a good life (achieving happiness) when she is performing the function of human beings well. To determine our function, Aristotle looks at what is special or unique about human beings, which is our rationality. Unlike other animals who can act only on instinct, we have reason, which enables us to reflect on our motivations and freely choose what to do. Aristotle defines our function as "an activity of soul which follows or implies a rational principle." The good person will perform this function well, and this implies she does it with virtue (or excellence). So Aristotle concludes that "happiness is an activity of soul in accordance with perfect virtue."[5]

Therefore, if we wish to understand the nature of happiness, we need to learn about virtue, which involves the state of a person's soul. Aristotle begins with the idea that "one element in the soul is irrational," and the other "has a rational principle," by which he means reason. Aristotle describes one part of the irrational element as vegetative in nature, meaning it governs our basic biological functioning that includes nutrition and growth. Since nonhuman animals also have this part of the soul, "it has by its nature no share in human excellence." However, he explains, "there seems to be another irrational element in the soul—one which in a sense, however, shares in a rational principle," and this part is unique to human beings. Aristotle describes this part as involving appetite and desire, and its job is to listen to the dictates of reason, which is trying to promote what is best for the person. In some people, this irrational part "fights against and resists this [rational] principle," but in the virtuous person, it listens to reason and "speaks, on all matters, with the same voice as the rational principle."[6]

Since there are two elements within the soul (the rational and irrational), there are two corresponding kinds of virtue, one relating to the intellect (intellectual virtue) and the other to one's character (moral virtue). Although Aristotle gives separate accounts of how to achieve each kind of virtue (intellectual and moral), Sarah Broadie argues that it is a mistake to think these two kinds of virtue can occur apart, for "excellences of character are impossible without the intellectual excellence which he calls 'phronesis,' often translated as 'practical wisdom.'"[7] Being virtuous implies that one is living well, but living well requires having both a good character and wisdom, for the "listening" part must follow the dictates of reason, but reason must also provide good commands. Therefore, happiness requires one to possess moral and intellectual virtue, both of which mutually reinforce each other.

However, Aristotle denies that having a virtuous soul is sufficient for happiness, because "it is impossible, or not easy, to do noble acts without the proper equipment." The virtuous person must also be "sufficiently equipped with external goods," such as money, health, an attractive physique, good friends and family, and a certain amount of good fortune. Aristotle explains, "The man who is very ugly in appearance or ill-born or solitary and childless is not very likely to be happy, and perhaps a man would be still less likely if he had thoroughly bad children or friends or had lost good children or friends by death. As we said, then, happiness seems to need this sort of prosperity in addition."[8]

Although Aristotle believes that virtue is necessary for happiness, his recognition of the importance of external factors (including luck) in achieving happiness marks a departure from the theorists we considered in the previous chapter, namely, Plato and the Stoics.[9] Reflection on our commonsense intuitions about happiness suggests Aristotle's view is more plausible. For instance, the virtuous person is supposed to exhibit good character traits, such as kindness, patience, and generosity. But how can one exhibit these traits if she is shunned by her society (as in Plato's example of the perfectly just man) or if she is destitute? I can be called a generous person only if I have demonstrated generosity, but this entails that I have enough to give and that I have someone to give it to. Although your poverty and lack of family may not be your fault or lie within your control, the absence of these goods will most certainly adversely affect your happiness.

Plato and the Stoics want happiness to be completely self-sufficient, meaning it is something that anyone can attain by virtue of her own merits. But as I suggested earlier, it is doubtful how many human beings could actually be happy without at least some measure of external goods. Even Aristotle reacts with what Annas calls "outraged common sense" when he considers Plato's example of the perfectly just man, for Aristotle charges, "Those who say that the victim on the rack or the man who falls into great misfortunes is happy if he is good are, whether they mean to or not, talking nonsense."[10] Aristotle's view of happiness provides a more accurate picture of human nature, and I suspect that is part of the reason Aristotle's view has had such a profound influence on contemporary philosophers' views of happiness.

Returning to the question of how we become virtuous, Aristotle tells us that intellectual virtue "owes its birth and its growth to teaching (for which reason it requires experience and time), while moral virtue comes about as a result of habit." In his work the *Nicomachean Ethics,* Aristotle spends considerably more time discussing moral virtue, which he argues does not arise in us naturally. We can always change our characters (and become more honest or generous), but we cannot change what arises in us by nature. According to Aristotle, we become morally good or bad people based on the habits we choose to cultivate, and he warns, "It makes no small difference, then, whether we form habits of one kind or another from our very youth; it makes a very great difference, or rather all the difference."[11]

Aristotle believes virtues are like other skills that we learn first by doing them. For instance, we become dancers by dancing, pianists by playing the piano, and chefs by cooking. Similarly, Aristotle says, "we become just by doing just acts, temperate by doing temperate acts, brave by doing brave acts."[12] However, what one must do in order to become virtuous cannot be prescribed exactly, for it will vary depending on the situation. One could draw a comparison with health: all healthy people are in the same physical state, but how much food and exercise they need to maintain their health will depend on the individual. Similarly, all virtuous people are in the same state, but what they must do to be brave or honest, for example, will vary.

All virtuous people do share something important: they avoid both excess and defect, and they strive for moderation in their feelings and actions. Once again, we can draw a comparison with health: if you eat or exercise too much (excess) or too little (defect), you will cease to be healthy, whereas the healthy person will get just the right (moderate) amount of food and exercise. Similarly, the person who feels too much fear will be cowardly, while the person who feels too little fear (or has too much confidence) will be rash. Being courageous implies that one experiences a moderate amount of fear or confidence, and Aristotle argues that all virtues involve moderation.

Therefore, your state of character determines how you experience your emotions and whether you feel them too strongly, too weakly, or just the right amount. Virtues are states of your character, which imply that you stand well with respect to your emotions, because you feel them moderately. Aristotle believes all emotions, which include fear, confidence, anger, appetite, pity, pleasure, and pain, could be felt too intensely or too weakly. The virtuous person will be disposed to feeling them "at the right times, with reference to the right objects, towards the right people, with the right motive, and in the right way."[13]

Aristotle's view implies that feeling our emotions moderately is essential for achieving virtue and living well, once again putting him at odds with the Stoics, who sought to minimize the influence of the emotions. The Stoics believe reason should control or eliminate one's emotions, and they equate virtuous behavior with acting solely on the dictates of reason. In contrast, Aristotle views the emotions as an essential part of reacting in the right way to a situation, and I believe Aristotle's view better reflects our commonsense intuitions.

Consider all the situations in which demonstrating an emotional response is not only expected, but required. One should grieve over the death of a spouse or child, for that is a healthy way of coping with the loss of someone who is cared about. The person who remains completely unaffected emotionally, who demonstrates no sadness or grief, might be deemed callous or suspected of not really loving or caring for the person who has died.[14]

Furthermore, psychologists have found that our "gut reactions" (which rely on our emotions without thinking) can be more accurate than our deeply analyzed responses, and this research challenges Plato's contention that reason is our best guide to living well. In one study, a group of people were asked to think about their current romantic relationships and provide a list of reasons to support their level of satisfaction or dissatisfaction.[15] People in another group were simply told to give their "gut reactions" to the relationships without doing any analysis. One would think the group who took the time to analyze their relationships would give more accurate answers about how they felt, but just the opposite was true. The satisfaction ratings of the group who gave their "gut reactions" predicted whether they were still dating their partners several months later, whereas the ratings of the analyzing group did not predict the outcome of their relationships at all. This study suggests too much analysis might confuse people about how they really feel. For instance, ignoring one's feelings and listening only to reason might cause one to stay in a relationship in which one is not happy, simply because (according to reason) things appear to be just fine. Aristotle's view recognizes the importance of our emotions in living well, a point that is not emphasized enough by either Plato or the Stoics.

Empirical research on happiness lends further support for Aristotle's contention that we develop a virtuous nature first by acting, for psychologists have found that asking study participants to go out and do something nice for someone caused the participants to view themselves as more kind and considerate people. As psychologist Timothy D. Wilson explains, "Numerous social psychological studies have confirmed Aristotle's observation that 'We become just by the practice of just actions, self-controlled by exercising self-control, and courageous by performing acts of courage.' If we are dissatisfied with some aspect of our lives, one of the best approaches is to act more like the person we want to be, rather than sitting around analyzing ourselves."[16]

Richard Taylor is a contemporary philosopher who presents a view of happiness similar to Aristotle's, and he argues that many people spend their lives pursuing the wrong ideals, missing out on happiness altogether. According to Taylor, we can test whether someone is happy by asking ourselves whether we would wish to be that other person; if we would not, then it must be because she is not really happy. Taylor suggests, "If someone seems to himself or herself to be happy, perhaps he or she really is happy after all. But one can see how shallow this is by asking whether one would really wish to *be* that other person. It is hard to see why not, if that other person is believed to be truly happy. But we know, in fact, that such persons are not; they only seem so to themselves, largely because they are unwilling to admit their own folly."[17]

Taylor defines happiness as the proper functioning of the person as a whole, and following Aristotle and the other ancient ethicists, he sees happiness as intimately connected with using reason or our natural intelligence. But Taylor advocates a broader conception of reason that includes "not merely the activity of reasoning (as exhibited for example in philosophy) but also observation and reflection and, above all, creative activity."[18] Therefore, on Taylor's view, happiness involves fulfilling ourselves as human beings by using our creative powers, which encompass the arts and any sort of activity that is guided by intelligence, such as dance, athletics, gardening, playing chess, rearing a family, or exercising skill at a profession or in business.

Now that we have considered all three historical sources as well as several contemporary philosophers who view virtue (which includes both our moral and our intellectual development) as a necessary condition for achieving happiness, we are ready to subject this view to critical analysis to see whether it is viable as a theory of happiness.

Is Virtue Necessary for Happiness?

The first problem that arises when we consider the identification of happiness with virtue is with the standard that must be met in order to deem someone happy. The objection is that by requiring one to fully develop her intellect and character before she can be said to be happy, this view sets the standard for achieving happiness too high. If we actually adopted this standard in our ordinary attributions of happiness, it seems very few people would qualify as happy. And given the difficulty in gauging the exact state of development of someone's intellect or character, we would have no practical way of applying this notion, and we could never confidently call anyone happy. I question the value of having such a word in our language.

Ordinarily, we do not need to examine the development of a person's intellect or character in order to know whether she is happy or unhappy, and we frequently make happiness attributions independent of the formal criteria advocated by these theorists.[19] Their view fails to represent the concept of happiness, and they seem to have taken a word from the ordinary person's lexicon and provided it with a philosophical definition that has lost its connection with the ordinary notion. We need an argument for why we should adopt the more stringent view of happiness found in philosophy, for without an argument demonstrating the superiority of the philosophical concept, we have no reason to accept the idea that virtue is necessary for achieving happiness.

Our ordinary use of *happiness* also permits us to talk about the happy baby or child, yet this would be impossible if we identify happiness with virtue, for babies and even children do not yet have the mental capacities necessary for achieving moral or intellectual virtue.[20] Aristotle and the ancient ethicists accept this implication, which is also acknowledged by Taylor, who argues that "children, idiots, barbarians, and even animals are perfectly capable of experiencing pleasure and pain, but none of these can become happy," because none can achieve happiness "in the sense that is important to philosophy, that is, in the sense of having achieved fulfillment or having been blessed with the highest personal good." Foot is also sympathetic to this implication, for she connects happiness with "what is deep in human nature."[21] Yet the restricted usage advocated by philosophers clearly deviates from the way ordinary people use the word *happiness.* Although a child may not be capable of achieving moral or intellectual virtue, or of connecting with what is deep in human nature, we often refer to children as experiencing happiness and unhappiness.

Furthermore, identifying happiness with virtue appears to misrepresent ordinary people's motivations and behavior. Modern society is replete with examples of happy immoralists, people who knowingly break the moral law and are unaffected by it.[22] As Bernard Williams notes, "There is also the figure, rarer perhaps than Callicles supposed, but real, who is horrible enough and not miserable at all but, by any ethological standard of the bright eye and the gleaming coat, dangerously flourishing."[23] We frequently make sense of people's behavior by referring to their belief that such behavior will increase their happiness, even when that behavior is immoral or self-destructive. If we cannot explain their motivation in terms of happiness, how can we make sense of why they act immorally?

Additional problems emerge when we take a closer look at Taylor's suggestion for evaluating the happiness of others. According to Taylor, my wanting (or not wanting) to be another person will determine whether that person is truly happy, but this view of happiness is completely mistaken. Consider an example. If I do not share your penchant for chocolate ice cream, I might not long to be you (while you are eating chocolate ice cream). However, my not wanting to be you says nothing about the quality of your experience or your mental state; it certainly has no bearing on the question of whether you are happy while eating your chocolate ice cream. My wanting or not wanting to be someone else is clearly a reflection of my values and preferences, but it says very little about the other person.

Furthermore, I might not want to be you because I have a moral objection to the source of your happiness. Perhaps you get pleasure from eating a juicy steak. I might not want to be you because I am a vegetarian who does not believe it is morally right to eat meat. The fact that I object to the source of your satisfaction should not detract from any happiness you might experience while eating your steak. Could I deny a person's experience of fear on the grounds that I do not find her particular situation scary? Could I deny someone else's hunger because I believe she has eaten enough? Obviously, what I feel (or what I suppose I would feel if I were in your shoes) has no bearing on your state of mind. The same reasoning applies to happiness. I cannot deny another person's satisfaction, because I would not be satisfied were I to be her.

Foot's remarks about happiness also raise objections, for she attempts to list the acceptable means for achieving happiness, which include "affection for children and friends, the desire to work, and love of freedom and truth."[24] But what about the person who is made miserable by her work, children, friends, or family? How can her happiness be tied to such things? Clearly, for some people happiness does come from Foot's sources, but for others, happiness may be linked to something else. Why should we limit the concept of happiness to only those sources Foot deems appropriate, when we are given no justification for her list over any other? Foot appears to be confusing some typical causes of happiness with the nature of happiness. For many people, satisfaction may arise from Foot's causes, but what typically causes happiness in some (or even most people) is conceptually distinct from the nature of happiness. Our collective experience suggests that when someone is in a state of satisfaction, she is happy, regardless of what caused her to be in that state.

The ancient ethicists have a history of conflating happiness with a person's well-being and her moral character, but this conflation changes the meaning of the word *happiness* and causes their theories to deviate from our ordinary understanding of this concept. I believe we are better served by recognizing the independence of a person's happiness, well-being, and moral character, for this arms us with much greater explanatory power, thus enabling us to discuss a wider range of actual cases. For instance, a person might take great satisfaction in the suffering of others, such that their suffering makes her happy. Recognizing this person's happiness does not preclude us from defending the moral judgment that she is a despicable person. In this case, it is the source of her happiness (that she gets satisfaction from the suffering of others) that actually supports our moral judgment.

One reason the ancient ethicists deem virtue a necessary condition for happiness is because they identify happiness with the greatest good. On their view, being happy implies that one is living "the good life," which requires one to develop the best characteristics of human beings, namely, moral and intellectual excellence. But we have no reason to accept their first step, which is to conflate happiness with the good life. If we separate the realm of happiness from the realm of morality, we can accept the immoralist's happiness without thereby committing ourselves to any particular view of the goodness of her life. That is, we can accept the immoralist's satisfaction while admonishing her for it.

Severing the connection between happiness and virtue better represents the way *happiness* functions in our language today, for being happy generally implies nothing about the moral worth of a person's life or her activities, and we often assess a person's happiness without knowing anything about her moral character. Yet recognizing the independence of happiness does not preclude us from issuing evaluative judgments, for we can still make judgments that appeal to other dimensions of people's lives, such as their moral character, well-being, fulfillment, religious devotion, or aesthetic sensibility. Put simply, we can recognize happiness as simply one good among many others.[25]

Perhaps someone who is sympathetic to the identification of happiness with virtue could offer a reply to my objections, for this person might insist that the whole point of identifying happiness with virtue is to revise our current concept of happiness, not to capture it. We know the masses think happiness comes from conventional goods like health and wealth, but it is the philosopher's job to tell us what happiness really is. Therefore, we cannot (and should not) look to common usage for help with understanding the nature of happiness.

Annas makes a similar argument about virtue, for she says our ordinary concept of virtue is rather weak and confused and that our understanding can be greatly improved by looking to the ancient philosophers. She also applies this reasoning to happiness, suggesting, "If we accept that our conception of happiness contains several different and incompatible elements, we may regard it as we do our conception of virtue and try to understand the ancient ideas as more coherent and stronger versions of the conception which we recognize as important but have lost consistent interpretation of."[26]

I believe Annas's mistake is assimilating happiness and virtue. I am willing to agree with Annas about virtue, for most people do not appear to have even the slightest idea what the term connotes—other than its connection with patience, perhaps—and we can learn a lot from the ancients about the nature of virtue and why it is good for us. As Annas suggests, thinking about virtue can encourage us to see life differently, for it can help to reorient our priorities and how we choose to live. But you cannot make the same argument with respect to happiness, because our ideas about happiness are neither vague nor ill-defined. Ask students their opinions about happiness, and a flurry of hands will shoot up. Mention happiness casually at a social gathering, and you will see how much people have to say on the matter. Of course, people's opinions will vary, but what you don't get is a blank stare.

Ordinary people with little or no philosophical training have plenty of robust intuitions about happiness, which is why one cannot just state (as Plato does) that the perfectly just man on the rack is happy, for our collective experience suggests otherwise. Virtue and even well-being are different, for they play no central role in the ordinary person's lexicon, and are, therefore, more amenable to being supplied with a technical or philosophical definition. Happiness is as important to the man on the street as it is to the philosopher, so the philosopher cannot simply redefine the term. Our shared understanding of happiness must constrain our philosophizing; otherwise, the philosophers will be vulnerable to the charge that they have changed the subject matter, and their theories will not be taken seriously.

In this chapter and the previous one, we considered the view that virtue is necessary for happiness, and we have found it objectionable. Although some people may achieve happiness through a life of virtue, there is nothing in the nature of happiness to suggest that it is necessary. We shall consider an altogether different approach to happiness in the next chapter, a view that is more reminiscent of hedonism, for it equates being happy with getting what you want or having your desires satisfied.

Notes

1. Aristotle, *Nicomachean Ethics,* translated by David Ross (Oxford: Oxford University Press, 1998), 1045a1–2.

2. Aristotle actually uses two different Greek words to refer to the condition of living and doing well—*eudaimonia* and *makarios.* However, following Annas, I shall treat both as referring to the same end state, which is happiness. As Annas explains, "'Blessed' (*makarios*) is a loftier and more pretentious word than 'happy' (*eudaimon*), but they are interchangeable (other than stylistically). Arius [the Stoic philosopher] says firmly that it makes no difference which word you use." Annas, *The Morality of Happiness* (New York: Oxford University Press, 1993), 44.

3. Aristotle, *Nicomachean Ethics,* 1097a17–22.

4. Ibid., 1097b22–28.

5. Ibid., 1095a8, 1102a5.

6. Ibid., 1102a28, 1102b12, 1102b12–15, 1102b17.

7. Aristotle, *Nicomachean Ethics,* translated by Sarah Broadie and Christopher Rowe (Oxford: Oxford University Press, 2002), 17.

8. Ibid., translated by Ross, 1099a30, 1101a15, 1099b3–7.

9. However, some commentators argue that Plato actually agrees with Aristotle that virtue is necessary but not sufficient for happiness and that it was Socrates (and the Stoics) who thought it was also sufficient. According to Gregory Vlastos, Plato views virtue as the main component of happiness, but he recognizes that there are other constituents as well. See Vlastos, *Socrates, Ironist and Moral Philosopher* (Ithaca, NY: Cornell University Press, 1991), chap. 8, esp. 204–205. Terence Irwin also supports this interpretation: "When Plato argues that the just person is in all circumstances happier than the unjust person, he does not imply that the just person is happy in all circumstances. He leaves open the possibility that happiness has components that are not infallibly secured by justice. . . . Plato gives no reason to deny that the external goods lost by the just person [in Glaucon's example] are genuine goods. . . . [H]e implicitly acknowledges that the just person suffers a significant loss in being deprived of external goods." Irwin, *Plato's Ethics* (New York: Oxford University Press, 1995), 192.

10. Julia Annas, "Should Virtue Make You Happy?," *Aepiron* 35 (2003): 11–12; Aristotle, *Nicomachean Ethics,* translated by Ross, 1153b16–22.

11. Aristotle, *Nicomachean Ethics,* translated by Ross, 1103a15–20, 1103b25.

12. Ibid., 1103b1.

13. Ibid., 1106b20.

14. However, William Irvine argues that it is a mistake to assume a good Stoic never grieves, for the Stoics understood that certain emotions are reflexive. Irvine explains, "Suppose, in particular, that a Stoic finds himself grieving over the loss of a loved one. This Stoic . . . will not react by trying to stifle the grief within him. . . . After this bout of reflexive grief, though, a Stoic will try to dispel whatever grief remains in him by trying to reason it out of existence." Irvine, *A Guide to the Good Life* (Oxford: Oxford University Press, 2009), 216.

15. Timothy D. Wilson, "Don't Think Twice, It's All Right," *New York Times,* December 29, 2005.

16. Ibid.

17. Richard Taylor, "Virtue Ethics," in *Happiness: Classic and Contemporary Readings in Philosophy,* edited by Steven M. Cahn and Christine Vitrano (New York: Oxford University Press, 2008), 224.

18. Ibid., 231.

19. My objection here challenges the necessity of achieving moral and intellectual virtue in happiness attributions. Raymond Belliotti also questions whether achieving moral and intellectual virtue is sufficient: "Imagine showing someone that they embodied the prescribed intellectual and moral virtues, and the conditions for faring well. Suppose the person agreed but still insisted, 'But I am not happy.' If we respond 'Oh, you are happy, you just don't know it,' our words are odd. If I don't know that I am happy, how can I be happy? . . . Without the appropriate state of mind, experience, or feelings, however, achieving Aristotle's condition of the self fails to capture the internal response necessary for happiness." Belliotti, *Happiness Is Overrated* (Lanham, MD: Rowman and Littlefield, 2004), 17. But see Richard Kraut, "Two Conceptions of Happiness," *Philosophical Review* 88 (1979): 167–197, who argues that anyone who meets Aristotle's standards for happiness would also be happy on our standard, because this person would automatically have the necessary positive attitude toward her life that we associate with happiness.

20. Actually, as Belliotti notes, Aristotle's view is even more restrictive, because "women, slaves, and most males could not be happy because they lacked, by virtue of their social positions or natures, the necessary intellectual ability or the conditions for faring well" (ibid., 13). However, Belliotti argues that Aristotle's convictions about the intellectual inferiority of women, slaves, and manual laborers could be dismissed while still appreciating his key insights about happiness (15).

21. Taylor, "Virtue Ethics," 111; Philippa Foot, *Moral Dilemmas* (Oxford: Clarendon Press, 2002), 35.

22. Of course, many ancient moralists would reject this description of the "happy immoralist" as a contradiction in terms, for they viewed acts of immorality as destructive of happiness. In *Good and Evil* (Amherst, NY: Prometheus Books, 2000), Richard Taylor aptly describes the ancients' view of the negative effects of injustice on a person: "Committing acts of injustice does corrupt . . . or make you morally worse; indeed, it is the very expression of such inner corruption. And because such corruption is . . . the corruption or ruin of your very soul—indeed, of your inner being—then it is the ruination of that which is to everyone the most precious of possessions. It is the dissolution of your very person" (85).

23. Bernard Williams, *Ethics and the Limits of Philosophy* (Cambridge, MA: Harvard University Press, 1985), 46.

24. Foot, *Moral Dilemmas,* 35.

25. Thomas Hurka reaches a similar conclusion in his recent book *The Best Things in Life* (New York: Oxford University Press, 2011), where he argues, "Contrary to Epicurus, Socrates, and many others, there isn't just one ultimate good—there are many. Pleasure isn't the only good thing in life, nor is philosophical understanding; each is just one item on a longer list of goods, so an ideal life can contain different good things" (6). See also Mike W. Martin's recent book *Happiness and the Good Life* (New York: Oxford University Press, 2012), where he suggests that "we are happy insofar as we love our lives, valuing them in ways manifested by ample enjoyments and a robust sense of meaning" and that we should view happiness as "one dimension of good lives interacting with other dimensions, in particular with authenticity, health, self-fulfillment, moral decency and goodness, and meaningfulness in terms of justified values" (3).

26. Julia Annas, "Virtue and Eudaimonism," in *Happiness,* edited by Cahn and Vitrano, 258.

CHAPTER FOUR

Happiness as Desire Satisfaction

Thus far, we have rejected two theories of happiness, one that identifies it with pleasure and the other with virtue, because their understanding of happiness was too restrictive, thereby making them vulnerable to counterexamples. We are interested in a theory of the nature of happiness; that is, we want to find the quality (or qualities) shared by all happy people or what it is they have in common. While some people can attribute their happiness to experiences of pleasure or to a virtuous character, neither quality is true of everyone who is happy, so neither can be part of the nature of happiness.

In the next three chapters, the search continues in a new direction with theories that focus on satisfaction as a key element of happiness. Satisfaction views of happiness are quite prevalent, especially within the contemporary literature, and all agree that satisfaction is a necessary condition for achieving happiness. The main issue that divides them is whether satisfaction is also sufficient for happiness or whether some additional conditions must also be met.

For simplicity, I have divided the satisfaction views into three different chapters. The theorists in this chapter all define satisfaction narrowly in terms of having your desires fulfilled. In contrast, the theorists in Chapters 5 and 6 use the term *satisfaction* more broadly, so that it refers to a person's mental state (and it is not limited strictly to the satisfaction of her desires).

The Simple Satisfaction View

According to the theorists in this chapter, happiness is achieved by seeking to maximally satisfy one's desires, and they are committed to the idea that a person's level of happiness will be proportional to the number of desires she is able to satisfy. I shall refer to this as the "simple satisfaction view," because it provides little explanation of the psychological state of happiness independent of its reduction to the gratification of a person's desires.

The simple satisfaction view is rarely justified by formal argument, and in this respect, it is similar to hedonism, which is also stated as if it were indisputable. I suspect many proponents of the simple satisfaction view are actually hedonists, because pleasure is often equated with the feeling that attends the gratification of desire. If pleasure is defined as having your desires satisfied, and happiness is defined in the same way, then happiness is nothing more than a state of pleasure, which commits one to hedonism. But one can certainly adopt the simple satisfaction view without endorsing any particular view of pleasure, and we have already discussed numerous problems associated with hedonism. Therefore, we shall evaluate the simple satisfaction view independently without assuming any connection with hedonism.

There are several formulations of the simple satisfaction view found within the contemporary literature. What unites them is their agreement that desire satisfaction is a necessary component of happiness. Where they differ is in the additional conditions they impose, which must be met if one is to be deemed happy. We shall begin with the simplest version in this section and then consider increasingly more complex versions in the sections that follow.

The least-complicated version of the simple satisfaction view is clearly stated by Masatoshi Matsushita: "We define happiness as the fulfillment of desires. When we are hungry, we desire to eat. If we succeed in eating, we are happy. When we want to love, we are happy if we find the right mates, etc. So happiness is the fulfillment of desires." Similarly, David Gauthier notes, "We may think of the happy man as the man who is able to satisfy his wants, or acquisitive desires." And Diane Jeske explains, "An agent is happy when she promotes what has subjective value for her," by which she means a person is happy when she is realizing all or many of her individual goals or desires.[1]

All three accounts identify happiness with getting what you want, and none imposes any further conditions that must be met in order for a person to be happy. We can summarize this view with the following thesis: a person's happiness level will be determined by the quantity of desires she is able to satisfy, with more satisfied desires leading to an increase in happiness and less to a decrease. When phrased in this way, however, there is an obvious problem, for this thesis appears to be false. There are many cases in which a person's happiness is completely unaffected by the number of desires she has satisfied (or the amount she has left unsatisfied). For example, there is no contradiction in imagining someone who has had all of her desires satisfied, yet who fails to be happy. Nor is there any problem with saying, "I got what I wanted, but I am still not happy." As James Griffin explains, "It is depressingly common that when even some of our strongest and most central desires are fulfilled, we are no better, even worse, off." Similarly, Jean Austin observes that "I may want something but not like it when I have got it," which leads her to conclude that "to like what one has got, rather than to get what one wants," is necessary for happiness.[2]

First, let us consider an example that demonstrates how someone may have a desire fulfilled yet fail to be happy. Joe is a writer who has sent his manuscript to ten publishers. His most important desire is to have his book accepted; however, he is becoming more doubtful with each new rejection he receives. Unbeknownst to Joe, the tenth publisher has decided to accept his book proposal. Unfortunately, the letter informing him of the good news has gotten lost in the mail. Although Joe's desire has actually been fulfilled, this achievement has had no effect on his state of happiness. Joe still feels anxiety combined with mild depression over all the rejections.

The simple satisfaction view implies that Joe should be happy, when it is obvious that he is not happy. This objection suggests it is the agent's perception of the fulfillment of her desire that is crucial for promoting her happiness, not just the act of fulfillment itself. Delivering the wrong verdict on Joe's case is a serious problem for the simple satisfaction view, because the situation depicted in this case is not exceptional. Any time a person's desires are satisfied without her knowledge, she will fail to be happy. Therefore, happiness must involve something more than just having your desires satisfied.

The Simple Satisfaction View: Second Formulation

In response to the objection raised above, theorists have included additional conditions besides desire satisfaction that must also be met if one is to be deemed happy. For instance, Wayne Davis offers a theory of happiness that involves belief, desire, and thinking. According to Davis, "To be happy is to be thinking, with respect to a bunch of things, that they are turning out as you want them to turn out."[3] To illustrate Davis's view, let us suppose at this moment I want to have a successful marriage and a secure career, and I do not care about anything else. According to Davis, I will be happy at this moment to the extent that I believe I have a successful marriage and a secure career, and the more strongly I want (and believe) these to be the case, the happier I will be. Davis defines happiness during a period of time as the average level of momentary happiness the person enjoyed during that time. So your happiness during the first five years of your marriage, for example, will be the average of whatever momentary happiness you experienced during those five years.

Davis also distinguishes between objective and subjective satisfaction of desires. According to Davis, my desires are objectively satisfied when I actually obtain whatever it is that I desire, even if I do not know that my desire has been satisfied. Subjective satisfaction will occur whenever I believe that my desires have been satisfied, even if I am mistaken. Davis argues that "happiness depends on the subjective satisfaction of desires, and at best only indirectly on their objective satisfaction."[4] He offers the example of someone who reads in the paper that his lottery ticket has won. Davis argues that this person will be ecstatic as long as he believes he is a lottery winner, even if what the newspaper printed was an error. Davis's view clearly improves on the previous version of the simple satisfaction view, for he makes happiness a function of a person's perception that she is getting what she wants. Because Davis factors in the extent to which she believes that she is getting what she wants, his view easily avoids the objection raised in the previous section.

Steven Luper presents a similar account, for he believes happiness has two components for ordinary people: the satisfaction of desires and the "*appreciation* of that satisfaction." Luper's account also avoids the objection raised in the previous section, for he requires not only that your desires are fulfilled, but that you consciously recognize and appreciate their fulfillment. As Luper explains, "Satisfying our desires is important, but so is the pleasant apprehension and appreciation of that satisfaction."[5]

Returning to the example involving Joe, the writer, since he does not know that his desire has been satisfied, he cannot appreciate that satisfaction or believe that it has occurred. So Joe fails to meet one of the requirements of happiness stipulated by Davis and Luper. Therefore, both accounts will issue the correct judgment on Joe's case, deeming him unhappy.

However, there are also problems with Davis's and Luper's version of the simple satisfaction view. These problems emerge when we consider cases in which a person has a desire for something that she recognizes is immoral or imprudent (bad for her personal well-being). Just as there were pleasures that one was happier avoiding, there are desires that would destroy a person's happiness should they be realized. Philosophers Richard Brandt and Jaegwon Kim describe this possibility: "A person may know that he wants p, but think it a bad thing that he does and refrain from doing what he thinks will lead to p."[6]

Let us consider an example to illustrate this problem. A Catholic priest may have a strong desire to become sexually involved with one of his parishioners, but he may also recognize that his desire is morally wrong according to the dictates of his religion. Acting to satisfy this desire will cost the priest his reputation and his livelihood; he will lose everything that he values and has spent his life trying to achieve. If the priest actually satisfies this desire, the consequences that follow will make the priest very unhappy. But according to Davis and Luper, happiness is nothing more than recognizing and appreciating that your desires are being satisfied. Therefore, Davis's and Luper's version of the simple satisfaction theory issues the wrong response to the priest's case, for his happiness is preserved by *not* acting to satisfy his desire.

Consider another case involving imprudent desires. Mark has recently suffered a massive heart attack that almost killed him. Doctors have told Mark that he must quit smoking, eat better, and start exercising or he will not live much longer. Mark is petrified by his prognosis, and this fear motivates him to adopt a healthier lifestyle. Unfortunately, old habits are hard to break, and our desires are not always within our control. Mark still experiences the craving to smoke and indulge in the unhealthy foods he used to enjoy, but he also realizes he is much happier by resisting these desires. Once again, Davis's and Luper's view issues the wrong judgment, for Mark would not be happier if he satisfied his imprudent desires.

The Simple Satisfaction View: Third Formulation

Robert Solomon offers a slightly more complex view that identifies happiness with being (and not merely feeling) satisfied. According to Solomon, one can be satisfied only when she procures the object of her desire. For instance, if my desire is to drink a glass of wine, I will be satisfied only when I drink some wine. But I can extinguish a desire without actually satisfying it, as when I drink a glass of soda instead of the wine. Extinguishing a desire leads to feeling (not being) satisfied. Solomon explains, "Both the gourmet and the dieter get rid of their hunger, but only the gourmet satisfies his hunger; the dieter extinguishes his."[7]

One may also feel satisfied when she falsely believes her desire has been fulfilled, but Solomon denies that one will be satisfied under such circumstances. Solomon argues that happiness is akin to being (not merely feeling) satisfied, because happiness is more "durable" and "eternal," while feelings are more transitory. Solomon offers an example: "I may feel satisfied . . . as I awake into a bright morning after a good night's sleep, momentarily unaware of the utterly miserable condition of my life and the utter frustration facing all my treasured desires. But this is not happiness, even if it is a very long good morning." Therefore, according to Solomon, "Happiness is not merely the satisfaction of one desire but the satisfaction of one's desires, not all or even most, but perhaps the most important of one's desires."[8]

Solomon's view is similar to the views of Davis and Luper in requiring the agent's conscious recognition that she has gotten what she wants, but he adds in another factor, which is that the desire also be important to the agent. This additional condition makes intuitive sense, for when we think about what makes a person happy or miserable, the important things certainly have more influence on a person's emotional state rather than the trivial. Simply satisfying trivial desires will not improve one's prospects for happiness if her important desires are being frustrated. For example, no matter how many trivial desires I am able to satisfy, they will have no effect on my happiness if I have just been diagnosed with incurable cancer or I have recently suffered the loss of a dear loved one.

Solomon's view avoids the objection raised in the previous section, because immoral and imprudent desires would not count as among one's most important desires. Although the priest wants to engage in a relationship with his parishioner, his desire to remain in the clergy and his desire to maintain his integrity are even more important. Similarly, although Mark wants to smoke cigarettes and eat fatty foods, his desire to avoid a premature death is more important. Therefore, Solomon's account delivers the correct verdict on both cases, for his view implies that satisfying immoral or imprudent desires will not increase one's happiness when those desires are for things that are unimportant.

Anthony Kenny describes happiness as "the satisfaction of one's major desires coupled with the belief that such satisfaction is likely to endure."[9] This sounds a lot like Solomon's view, but Kenny does not believe the satisfaction of one's desires automatically contributes to happiness, because we must also factor in the nature of the desires. He offers an example: consider the person whose only concern is to procure heroin, and he is able to obtain regular and safe supplies of the drug. Kenny is reluctant to call this person happy, even though his desire is being satisfied, because the nature of the desire suggests he is not living a rich and fulfilling life, which Kenny believes is also necessary for happiness.

Kenny argues that it is the combination of these two factors, contentment and richness, that leads to a paradox in the concept of happiness. He explains, "The greater a person's education and sensitivity, the greater his capacity for 'higher' pleasures and therefore for a richer life; yet increase in education and sensitivity brings with it an increase in the number of desires, and a corresponding lesser likelihood of their satisfaction. Instruction and emancipation in one way favour happiness and in another militate against it. To increase a person's chances of happiness, in the sense of fullness of life, is eo ipso [by that very act] to decrease his chances of happiness, in the sense of satisfaction of desire."[10]

Richard Warner's account is very similar to Kenny's, for he believes being happy involves meeting four conditions that are each necessary and, when taken together, are jointly sufficient for leading a happy life. According to Warner, one is leading a happy life if (1) her important desires are being satisfied sufficiently often, (2) she believes they are being satisfied, (3) she enjoys their satisfaction, and (4) she believes her desires are worthy.[11] Both Kenny and Warner agree that merely satisfying one's desire will not automatically contribute to happiness, for one must also factor in the nature of that desire. Both accounts are able to avoid the objections raised in the previous section that involved immoral and imprudent desires, because these kinds of desires clearly do not help one achieve a rich and fulfilling life, and no one would view such desires as worthy.

However, there are other cases that do present a problem for the more complex versions of the simple satisfaction view presented by Solomon, Kenny, and Warner. First, let us consider Sue, an aspiring actress who has always desired fame. After years of struggling, Sue has finally been given the lead role on a popular soap opera, and she is an overnight sensation. But as time passes, she grows increasingly more dissatisfied with her life. Although she now has all that she wanted, including steady work, recognition, money, and fame, she finds that she is not happy.

Sue's unhappiness is neither mysterious nor inexplicable; she simply misjudged what sort of lifestyle would suit her, as people often do. Sue thought she wanted money and fame, but upon attaining them, she realized she was much happier with her life of obscurity. She had more freedom then and more time to enjoy her free time without being harassed by adoring fans. She could not have anticipated these feelings about her new life, and it was only upon achieving fame that she realized how much it did not suit her.

All three views would imply that Sue is happy despite her own testimony that she is not. Furthermore, none of these views can provide an explanation for Sue's unhappiness, because she meets all of their conditions for happiness. Sue's most important desires have been fulfilled, and she consciously recognizes and appreciates that fulfillment. Furthermore, Sue's desire to be a successful actress is not defective in any obvious way; this desire could have made her life rich and fulfilling, and it was certainly worthy. The problem is not with the nature of the desire, but rather with Sue's reaction to the satisfaction of her desire. This example highlights the truth of the old adage, "Be careful what you wish for, it may actually come true." Or as George Bernard Shaw explains, "There are two tragedies in life. One is to lose our heart's desire. The other is to gain it."[12]

Sue's unhappiness clearly illustrates a weakness shared by all versions of the simple satisfaction view, which is the possibility that having your desires fulfilled can fail to make you happy. Our present desires involve predictions about how we will feel in the future, but whether we will actually feel satisfied when they are fulfilled will depend on the quality of our predictions. In some cases, predicting our future reactions is easy, as when I want my routine blood tests or a biopsy to come back normal. But in many other cases, it is much harder to appreciate how getting what you really want will change your life.

Psychologists have been studying our ability to predict our future emotional states, and they have found there are many situations in which people are prone to making errors in their judgments. As psychologists George Loewenstein and David Schkade explain, "There do, however, appear to be many situations in which people systematically mispredict their own future feelings. Besides marrying too young, there is shopping for groceries on an empty stomach; professing love during moments of lust; believing that one can eat 'just one chip'; deciding during the winter to vacation in the south during the summer; and believing that one could live the 'good life' if one's income were only 10 percent higher."[13] In situations where the subject's desires go awry in this way, simply fulfilling them will not increase happiness and may even lead to an increase in unhappiness. The simple satisfaction view will mishandle all cases like these.

Another problem case for Solomon, Kenny, and Warner arises when the subject wants something for reasons that are independent of its contribution to her happiness. Brandt and Kim describe the diversity in people's motivations by noting that when someone wants something, it does not imply that thing is wanted *for itself.* "Among the things a person can want is that he himself do a certain thing, but we should notice that a person can be motivated, e.g., by considerations of duty, to do something we should not say he wanted to do."[14]

Let us consider a case that illustrates this possibility. John comes from a military family. While he is in college, his country is attacked by terrorists and enters into a war. John decides to drop out of college and enlist in the army, but he does not want to join because he thinks it will make him happy. Rather, he believes it is his obligation to volunteer to protect his country. John recognizes that he will probably dislike being in the army, given his weak constitution and low tolerance for pain and discomfort. However, John still wishes to join the army, even knowing that he may be sacrificing his future happiness as a result. Let us suppose that after joining the army, John is quite miserable. He misses college, his family, and the comforts of his old life. He feels lonely and isolated in this foreign country where he is now stationed. Although John does not regret joining, for he believes he is making a positive contribution to the war effort, he is counting the days until he can return home.

According to the simple satisfaction view, John's decision to join the army, which satisfied his most important desire, should have made him happy, or at least caused some increase in his happiness. John obviously meets all of the criteria stipulated by Solomon's, Kenny's, and Warner's views, for he appreciates that his important and worthwhile desire has been satisfied. Yet John is miserable in the army, and his unhappiness was caused by the satisfaction of his desire.

There is one additional problem case for Solomon, Kenny, and Warner, which centers on the possibility that the cause of your happiness may have nothing to do with the fulfillment of your desires. The simple satisfaction view is unable to explain the effect of pleasant surprises, lucky breaks, and random occurrences of good fortune, which often increase one's happiness. For example, if my department chairperson tells me I have won an award, though I had no idea this award existed or that I had been nominated, my happiness is inexplicable on the simple satisfaction view, because it cannot be attributed to the satisfaction of an antecedent desire. Furthermore, the reason many pleasant surprises increase our happiness is precisely because they were not things we previously wanted or expected. For example, if your husband surprises you with flowers on a random weeknight, you might enjoy them even more than when you were expecting to receive them on a special occasion.

The same reasoning applies to instances of bad luck and misfortune, which often decrease happiness even when they are unrelated to any antecedent desires. Suppose your boss at work announces that your colleague has been chosen to receive a large bonus check. You might feel disappointed at not having been chosen even if you had no prior knowledge that such bonus checks were given out. Your unhappiness in this case cannot be attributed to the frustration of a desire, because you had no previous desire to win, even though after losing to your colleague, you now find yourself very unhappy.

The Simple Satisfaction View: Final Formulation

There is one final version of the simple satisfaction view to consider, which attempts to accommodate pleasant surprises and other experiences of good fortune. This view is proposed by V. J. McGill, whose book aims at explaining the controversy over happiness. McGill suggests that philosophers often appear to be giving very different definitions of happiness, which causes us to question whether they are even talking about the same concept. This is a problem, because if philosophers are talking about different concepts, they are not actually disagreeing with each other, and there will be no controversy over happiness to examine. In response, McGill argues that "each of these definitions [of happiness] is a particular refinement of a root meaning which is shared by those who give diverse definitions of it." McGill defines the root meaning of happiness as "a lasting state of affairs in which the most favorable ratio of satisfied desires to desires is realized, with the proviso that the satisfied desires can include satisfactions that are not preceded by specific desires for them, but come by surprise."[15]

Although McGill's view succeeds in avoiding the objection based on pleasant surprises, it still issues the wrong verdict on the cases involving Sue, the actress who desired fame, and John, the man who joined the army out of a sense of duty. The ratio of satisfied desires to desires is quite favorable for both Sue and John, for Sue has attained the fame and success she had desired, while John is fulfilling his desire to defend his country by fighting in a war abroad. McGill's view implies both Sue and John should be happy, when both are not. McGill's view, like the others we have already rejected, will issue the wrong verdict whenever someone like Sue misjudges what she wants. It will also mishandle cases like John's in which a person desires something for reasons completely unrelated to his own happiness.

The weakness of McGill's view, like all of those we have considered in this chapter, is the reliance on desire satisfaction in the definition of happiness. Even the most sophisticated versions of the simple satisfaction view fail to explain many fairly ordinary experiences of happiness and unhappiness. The problem appears to be related to the identification of happiness with desire satisfaction, for no matter how many conditions one adds, counterexamples still emerge. The counterexamples challenge the simple satisfaction theorist's main thesis by showing that desire fulfillment is neither necessary nor sufficient for happiness. It is not necessary, because one can be made happy by pleasant surprises and other gifts of fortune that one did not previously desire. And it is not sufficient, because one can get what she wants, yet still fail to be happy. Therefore, we ought to reject the simple satisfaction view as a theory of happiness.

I suspect the temptation to reduce happiness to the fulfillment of desire is due to the similarity of the emotions typically attending both. We often feel satisfied when we get what we want and dissatisfied when our desires are frustrated. The problem is that *happiness* has uses that extend beyond getting what one wants, as we have seen. The simple satisfaction theorist has made the same mistake as the hedonist, for she confuses one possible source of happiness with its nature. But just as we are often happy in the presence of displeasure, we are also happy in the absence of having our desires satisfied.

Notice, the proviso McGill includes is able to meet the pleasant-surprise objection, precisely because it sheds the commitment to the simple satisfaction view, relying instead on satisfaction construed more broadly. The theories we shall consider in the next chapter improve on the simple satisfaction view by avoiding talk of desire satisfaction altogether and instead identify happiness with feelings of satisfaction.

Notes

1. Masatoshi Matsushita, "Happiness and the Idea of Happiness," in *The Good Life and Its Pursuit*, edited by Jude Dougherty (New York: Paragon House, 1984), 47; David Gauthier, "Progress and Happiness: A Utilitarian Reconsideration," *Ethics* 78 (1967): 79; Diane Jeske, "Perfection, Happiness, and Duties to Self," *American Philosophical Quarterly* 33 (1996): 268, 270.

2. James Griffin, *Well-Being* (Oxford: Clarendon Press, 1986), 10; Jean Austin, "Pleasure and Happiness," *Philosophy* 43 (1968): 56.

3. Wayne Davis, "A Theory of Happiness," *American Philosophical Quarterly* 18 (1981): 113.

4. Ibid., 116.

5. Steven Luper, *Invulnerability: On Securing Happiness* (Chicago: Open Court, 1996), 37–38, 42.

6. Richard Brandt and Jaegwon Kim, "Wants as Explanations for Actions," *Journal of Philosophy* 60 (1963): 432.

7. Robert Solomon, "Is There Happiness After Death?," *Philosophy* 51 (1976): 191.

8. Ibid., 192.

9. Anthony Kenny, "Happiness," *Proceedings of the Aristotelian Society* 66 (1965–1966): 102.

10. Ibid.

11. Richard Warner, *Freedom, Enjoyment, and Happiness: An Essay on Moral Psychology* (Ithaca, NY: Cornell University Press, 1987).

12. George Loewenstein and David Schkade, "Wouldn't It Be Nice? Predicting Future Feelings," in *Well-Being: The Foundations of Hedonic Psychology*, edited by Daniel Kahneman, Ed Diener, and Norbert Schwarz (New York: Russell Sage Foundation, 2003), 85.

13. Ibid., 86.

14. Brandt and Kim, "Wants as Explanations for Actions," 426.

15. V. J. McGill, *The Idea of Happiness* (New York: Frederick A. Praeger, 1967), 5.

CHAPTER FIVE

Happiness as Something More than Satisfaction

The theorists we shall discuss in this chapter and in Chapter 6 solve the problems affecting the simple satisfaction view by correctly identifying happiness with feelings of satisfaction. They all agree that happiness is a psychological or mental state of the individual, not a state of affairs in the world, such as having your desires satisfied. Identifying happiness with a mental state of satisfaction is supported by common usage. For example, it would be difficult to understand someone who said, "I am completely dissatisfied with my life, yet I am no less happy for it," or "I am satisfied with everything that is important to me, yet I am so unhappy." In either case, we would suspect the person did not possess the concept *happiness* or had something pathologically wrong, because these statements are contradictory.

The theorists in both Chapters 5 and 6 agree that being satisfied with your life is a necessary condition of happiness; their main disagreement lies in whether it is sufficient. The theorists in this chapter believe that it is not, which leads them to include various conditions that must be met (in addition to satisfaction) if one is to be deemed happy. In contrast, the theorists in Chapter 6 believe being satisfied with your life is both necessary and sufficient for happiness.

I shall divide the theories in this chapter into two groups, based on the stringency of the standards they invoke in judging a person's happiness. I shall consider the group with the most restrictive evaluative standards first and show the incoherence of holding this view of happiness. Then I shall argue that even the more moderate evaluative view of happiness is indefensible.

The Normative View

John Kekes describes happiness as lasting satisfaction with one's life as a whole, which he regards as a central and noncontroversial aspect of happiness. He offers the following description of the happy person:

> Those who enjoy this satisfaction want their lives to continue by and large the same way; if asked, they would say that things are going well for them; their most important wants are being satisfied; they are doing and having much of what they want; they frequently experience joy, contentment, and pleasure; they are not divided about their lives; they are not often beset by fundamental inner conflicts; they are not given to lasting depression, anxiety, or frustration; they have no serious regrets about important decisions they have taken; nor are they ruled by such negative feelings as resentment, rage, envy, guilt, shame or jealousy.[1]

Kekes is offering a description of the mental state of satisfaction a person is in when she is happy. One might be alarmed by Kekes's reference to "getting what you want," which is reminiscent of the simple satisfaction view we just rejected. Unfortunately, several theories in this chapter make some reference to desire satisfaction. For instance, Richard Kraut describes someone as living happily when "he is very glad to be alive; he judges that on balance his deepest desires are being satisfied and that the circumstances of his life are turning out well."[2] However, the theories in this chapter are not vulnerable to the objections we raised against the simple satisfaction view, because they do not reduce happiness to desire satisfaction. Rather, they believe happiness is a mental state of satisfaction. Therefore, we should not get bogged down by their unfortunate choice of terminology and focus instead on the question of whether happiness should be identified with the mental state of satisfaction, or with something else.

Although the theorists in this chapter agree that being in a state of satisfaction with one's life is necessary for happiness, they deny that it is sufficient, for they believe in addition to being satisfied, one must also meet certain normative requirements in order to be judged happy. These normative requirements take into consideration factors such as the causal origin of one's state of satisfaction. I refer to this view as "normative" because these theorists believe happiness is governed by norms that can be invoked in order to criticize or correct a person's sincere report of happiness. According to the theorists in this chapter, one may believe that she is happy and be mistaken. For instance, if a person fails to achieve happiness in a way these theorists deem appropriate, if she fails to meet one of their requirements for happiness, then although she may believe that she is happy, she will not be. As Jean Austin explains, "To state that a man is happy is to assess his total condition, of which of course his own reactions to his condition are a part." The normative theorist believes the assessment of a person's happiness "must be in accordance with the standards accepted by the society in which he lives and precludes outrages to these."[3]

The normative view of happiness contrasts sharply with the life-satisfaction view we shall discuss in the next chapter. According to the life-satisfaction view, calling someone happy implies only that she is in a certain mental state, namely, one of satisfaction or contentment with her life; the life-satisfaction view says nothing about how or why she is in that state. According to the life-satisfaction view, there is no necessary connection between a person's happiness and actual events occurring in the world, and a person could be radically deceived about the most important aspects of her life and still be happy as long as she is satisfied with her life.

The normative theorist would object to the life-satisfaction view, because it provides no way to distinguish the happy person who is deluded, drugged, or in a virtual reality machine from the person who has a justified reason for being happy. By severing the external connection between one's state of happiness and events occurring in the world, the life-satisfaction view must deem all of these people as happy, even if their satisfaction is completely unjustified by the actual conditions of their lives.

One way to explain the difference between the life-satisfaction view and that of the normative theorist is that the life-satisfaction view considers statements about happiness to be akin to reports that describe a person's mental state. For example, if Joe reports that he is thirsty, one could not correct him by saying, "No, you're not; you've already had enough to drink." One cannot correct or falsify Joe's firsthand report, so long as he knows what *thirsty* means and speaks truthfully. The life-satisfaction theorist believes happiness functions similarly; if a person issues an honest report that she is happy, it is sufficient for her being happy, so long as she possesses the concept and speaks the truth. The life-satisfaction theorist believes a person's happiness is not something about which she can be mistaken.

In contrast, the normative theorist believes that when someone says she is happy, she is issuing an appraisal or making an evaluative judgment. Evaluative judgments involve meeting certain standards that don't apply to mere reports. For instance, when a judgment is issued, like "It is cold in here" or "That is a beautiful vase," certain standards are employed. One could challenge a judgment on the grounds that the requisite standard is not being met, thereby falsifying the judgment. The normative theorist believes one must meet certain standards in order to be happy. Although they differ on the nature and stringency of those standards, all normative theorists agree that a subject's report of her happiness is not sufficient for her being happy.

Happiness as Appraisal: First Formulation

We shall begin with R. M. Hare, whose writing on happiness provides a clear statement of the normative view. According to Hare, when one person calls another happy, "there is a rather complicated process of appraisal going on," because "the person who is making the judgment is appraising the life of the other person; but not entirely from the speaker's own point of view."[4]

When we say that someone is happy, we appraise her life using her standards, and not our own. For example, if I am a chef and you happen to hate to cook, you should attempt to adopt my view of cooking before you make a judgment about whether I am happy as a chef. To conclude that I am unhappy simply because you hate to cook is clearly inappropriate. Hare realizes the speaker's interests may differ greatly from the person whose happiness is in question. If happiness judgments were made entirely from the speaker's point of view, Hare would have to accept the ridiculous conclusion from the chef example. Instead, he explains, "Deciding whether to call somebody else happy is an exercise of the imagination."[5] In judging your happiness, I must imagine myself in your shoes, with your tastes and preferences. For example, although the squire may like to hunt animals for sport, an activity I do not enjoy, I can still recognize his happiness without implying that I would be happy living his life.

However, Hare does place a restriction on the type of preferences that should be factored in when judging happiness. Hare allows attributions of happiness to occur only in cases where we, the speaker, approve of the source of the subject's satisfaction. If the subject engages in an activity we find repulsive but the subject finds quite satisfying, Hare believes we should deny his happiness. To support this contention, Hare introduces the case of the "mental defective," a person who is capable of appreciating only the most basic pleasures and pains. If we imagine this person is able to get what he wants and avoid what he dislikes, should we say the mental defective is happy? Hare's reply is that we should deny his happiness, because we can appreciate all that he is missing. "We should think how much we enjoy all kinds of things like playing chess, which he can never know; and so we should be inclined to say 'He's not really happy' or 'He's not happy in the fullest sense of the word.'"[6]

Therefore, according to Hare, a person's satisfaction with her life is not sufficient for her happiness. The cause of that satisfaction must also be considered before we can say that she is happy, for one must partake in the right sorts of activities. Hare's reasoning is as follows: "Since what we have to do is to make an appraisal, not a statement of fact, we cannot content ourselves with merely recording how *he* appraises his life from *his* point of view; we have ourselves to make an appraisal, not merely to report on somebody else's appraisal."[7]

J. J. C. Smart expresses a similar intuition about happiness when he says, "To call a person 'happy' is to say more than that he is contented for most of the time. . . . It is, I think, in part to express a favorable attitude to the idea of such a form of contentment and enjoyment. That is, for A to call B 'happy,' A must be contented at the prospect of B being in his present state of mind and at the prospect of A himself, should the opportunity arise, enjoying that sort of state of mind."[8] Smart agrees with Hare about the evaluative nature of happiness, for when we call someone happy, we are not just reporting on that person's state of mind, but also endorsing her satisfaction.

However, Smart believes that happiness is both evaluative and descriptive. Smart argues that happiness has a descriptive component, because it is absurd to call someone happy who is in pain, not enjoying herself, or extremely dissatisfied with her life. To call someone happy is (at least in part) to describe that person's state of mind. Smart suggests that happiness involves enjoyment at various times the way a wet climate involves rain at various times, and he believes it is a necessary condition of happiness that the subject "be fairly contented and moderately enjoying himself for much of the time."[9]

Robert Simpson describes a person's satisfaction in terms of doing or getting whatever it is that she believes to be worthwhile. He believes this is a necessary but not sufficient condition of happiness, because in addition to being successful at pursuing one's ends, those ends themselves must also be worthwhile. Therefore, if one were to find satisfaction doing some meaningless task, one could not be considered happy on Simpson's view, because it is not a worthy end. Simpson explains that "a man may be prepared to claim of himself that he is happy, that he has what he wants in life, and the evidence of his appearance and behavior may be entirely consistent with this . . . but such evidence alone will not entitle us to call him happy, if we can make no favorable objective judgment on the worthwhileness of the activities in which his energy is spent."[10] Simpson's view of happiness is similar to that of Hare and Smart, because he also includes an evaluative component. Before issuing a judgment on a person's happiness, we must first consider the causal origin of her satisfaction. Should a person fail to partake in the right sorts of activities, Simpson would deny her happiness, regardless of how enjoyable she finds those activities.

Lynne McFall describes happiness as having a stable disposition to affirm one's life, but she argues that the subject must also be "leading . . . a life worth affirming (judged by some standard which is itself justified)." According to McFall, happiness involves judging "(1) that the set of one's important desires is (a) satisfied and (b) successful, and (2) to be satisfied as a consequence." However, simply issuing this judgment is not sufficient, because it must also be justified, meaning "it meets the requirements of rationality."[11] Like Smart, McFall's view of happiness employs both an evaluative and a descriptive standard. The descriptive standard involves the subject's satisfaction, which McFall refers to as having the set of one's important desires satisfied. But this condition is not sufficient, because happiness also has an evaluative component, which requires that a person's desires actually be satisfied and successful. A desire is successful when the subject views that desire as good. Therefore, McFall's account implies that being happy requires a person to be satisfied with her life, because she believes that her desires are both satisfied and good, and this belief must also be true.

According to McFall, if the subject's satisfaction with her life is not rationally justified, she will fail to be happy regardless of how satisfied she feels. Like the other normative theorists we have discussed, McFall must deny the subject's first-person authority over her own happiness. Although the subject may believe that she is satisfied with her life, she will be mistaken if her happiness is not rationally justified. McFall's view also implies that happiness is not attainable by everyone, for not all people possess the requisite mental capacities needed to meet the evaluative standard for happiness. For instance, McFall describes "the happy idiot" as someone who is incapable of achieving happiness, because she cannot justifiably affirm her life.[12]

All normative theorists agree that being satisfied with your life is a necessary condition of happiness, but they deny that it is sufficient, because happiness also requires meeting certain normative standards. The question we must address is whether the imposition of these standards is appropriate. I shall argue that the normative view is an implausible conception of happiness, because statements of happiness cannot be seen as evaluative judgments that invoke certain criteria, such as having "worthwhile" or rationally defensible goals or desires. I shall direct my criticism mainly at the account presented by Hare, because it provides the most detail; however, these objections apply to all of the theorists we have just discussed.

Let us begin with the normative theorist's claim that judgments of happiness involve some sort of appraisal. According to Hare, there are two types of cases: there are cases where we adopt the values of the subject, and there are cases where we find her values objectionable, thus leading us to deny her happiness. In the cases of the squire who likes hunting and shooting and the chef who enjoys cooking, we are supposed to adopt the subject's perspective, even though it may be different from our own, and declare these people happy. However, in the case of the mental defective, given his impoverished life, we should deny his happiness.

The problem is how we are to differentiate between these two sorts of cases. If Hare is willing to grant the squire's happiness, even though we wouldn't be happy if we had his life, why shouldn't the same reasoning apply to the mental defective? Both have personal preferences that we, the speakers, don't share. However, as Hare readily admits in the case of the squire, our preferences are completely irrelevant to the question of his happiness. But the same reasoning should apply to the case of the mental defective.

I believe drawing a distinction between these two kinds of cases introduces bias into happiness judgments that leads to all sorts of ridiculous conclusions. The same justification used to deny the happiness of the mental defective could be used to deny the happiness of any one of us who makes choices in life others don't endorse. For example, if a person chooses to remain single or childless, the speaker would be justified in saying, "Look at what you're missing!" and deny your happiness. But why should the decision not to get married or have children necessarily make you unhappy, simply because it is a choice the speaker doesn't endorse?

Furthermore, what can we say about all of the cases that straddle the line between the squire and the mental defective? How will we know whose values to adopt in cases involving a "mental defective" who loves music or who focuses single-mindedly on theoretical physics or mathematics? What about people who spend their time watching sports, like football or golf? What should we say about the professional bowler, actor, or supermodel? Are these activities as worthwhile as hunting and chess, where we should adopt the speaker's perspective, or do they push one into the mental defective's category, causing us to deny their happiness? It is not clear how we are to determine when someone is really happy "in the fullest sense of the word" and when we should say, "He's not really happy." The normative theorist simply assumes that everyone will agree on which activities are worthy and which are objectionable, but as these examples suggest, there are many cases that straddle the line, and unfortunately, these normative theorists do not offer us any guidance on how to differentiate between them.

These problems arise because of the normative standards, which permit a third party to revert to her own values in judging other people's happiness. The use of these standards turns happiness into an idiosyncratic concept, which tells us nothing informative about the subject's own state of mind. Happiness judgments become descriptions of the speaker's likes and dislikes and do not reflect the subject or her values. But this is a far cry from the concept of happiness with which we began, and it clearly does not reflect the way in which we use the word *happiness* today. Ordinarily, when I call someone happy, I am saying something important about how she feels about her life, which reflects her own values and preferences, and not my own.

According to Hare, the example of the squire demonstrates why happiness judgments should not be made "entirely from the speaker's own point of view." The squire is happy because "that is how *he* likes to live."[13] The squire example clearly shows why it is inappropriate to invoke the speaker's values when judging the happiness of someone else. Yet Hare's analysis of the mental defective contradicts this insight with the squire and turns happiness into an arbitrary notion that is useless for practical purposes.

Hare attempts to justify the distinction between the case of the squire and the mental defective by appealing to the speaker's power of imagination. If I can successfully view the world through your eyes, as in the case of the squire, then I can appreciate how you could be happy doing things that I might not enjoy. The mental defective is supposed to have values and interests that are so impoverished that no sane person would ever want to take on such a perspective. Therefore, Hare believes we should conclude that the mental defective is incapable of being happy.

However, reliance on "the powers of imagination" as a justification for distinguishing between these two cases is problematic. Clearly, people will differ in their ability to empathize, and this will lead to vast differences in their happiness judgments. For example, if I am a strict vegan who believes in animal rights, I will not be able to imagine how someone can enjoy killing small animals for fun, because I will view this form of entertainment as revolting and sadistic. In this case, I will not be able to say that the squire is happy, yet Hare, who has no problem jumping into the squire's shoes, readily grants the squire's happiness. But whose judgment of the squire's happiness is correct—mine or Hare's? Furthermore, why should the squire's happiness be determined by something as arbitrary as the speaker's own power of imagination? If the squire (or the chef, supermodel, professional golfer, or mental defective) is satisfied with his life, why isn't that enough to establish his happiness? It is not clear why third parties should be allowed to defeat the subject's own claim to happiness.

The normative theorist may offer a reply to this objection. As Hare suggests, "It is not lack of imagination that makes us unwilling to call him [the mental defective] really happy," but it is our *aversion* to doing so. It is this collective "aversion" that is supposed to justify why we should deny the happiness of one (the mental defective), but not another (the squire).

But this line of defense does no more to help the normative theorist than the reliance on people's fickle imaginations. Who says I will be averse to the "right things" (like the life of the mental defective) and not to the wrong ones (like hunting for sport)? Once again, we are left with the possibility of con-flicting and idiosyncratic judgments of happiness, for the speaker will be in-fluenced by her own beliefs and values when judging whether to be "averse" to those of the subject. These problems suggest that the normative theorist's claim that happiness has both an evaluative and a descriptive component is not warranted, and we ought to drop the normative constraints on when a person is happy. Without universal agreement about what is to count as a good life, or what are the worthwhile ways to spend one's time, the normative theorist is left with no justification for attributing happiness in some cases and denying it in others. By imposing such restrictive normative constraints on happiness, these theorists distort our ordinary concept of happiness and render it useless.

Happiness as Appraisal: Second Formulation

We must now consider the remaining theorists who hold a normative view of happiness, but who seek to impose upon it less stringent standards. I shall begin with Richard Kraut's view, which has been described as "the most widely dis-cussed contemporary philosophical treatment of happiness."[14] Kraut agrees with the other normative theorists that happiness is not purely descriptive, for reports of happiness also present positive evaluations of people's lives. Kraut argues against the view of happiness that he refers to as "extreme subjectivism," which says that "happiness is a psychological state and nothing more; it involves, among other things, the belief that one is getting the important things one wants, as well as certain pleasant affects that normally go along with this belief."[15] The life-satisfaction view would be an example of the kind of extreme subjectivism Kraut rejects, for it permits someone to be judged happy as long as she is satisfied with her life, regardless of whether her satisfaction is warranted or justified.

Kraut objects to extreme subjectivism, because he does not believe a person's sincere report of being happy is sufficient for happiness. Instead, he believes when we call someone happy, we are issuing an appraisal, which implies that her life meets certain standards. However, Kraut also rejects the more stringent normative view we just considered, because he believes the standards relevant for judging happiness ought to be determined by the subject and her personal goals. As Kraut explains, "For a person to be living happily, or to have a happy life, he must attain all the important things he values, or he must come reasonably close to this standard." This is not the only condition of happiness, for "one must also find that the things one values are genuinely rewarding, and not merely the best of a bad range of alternatives."[16]

Therefore, according to Kraut, when a person says that she is happy, she is issuing a positive appraisal of her life, which implies that she is satisfied because she is doing or getting whatever it is that she sees as worthwhile. Although being in this state of satisfaction is necessary for happiness, it is not sufficient, because "one can feel happy with one's life even if one comes nowhere near this goal; one need only believe that one is meeting one's standard."[17] To rule out such cases of misperception, Kraut introduces the additional condition that a person's belief that she is happy must be justified. The normative element of Kraut's view emerges with this condition, because the question of whether someone is meeting her own standard can be judged by anyone, and the subject does not possess first-person authority when judging her own happiness. If she fails to meet her own standards of happiness, then she will fail to be happy, regardless of how positively she feels about her life.

For example, let us say that Jane is perfectly satisfied with her life, because she believes that she has a successful marriage. However, Jane is terribly mistaken, because her husband is having an affair with his secretary. Given these circumstances, Kraut would say that Jane is not happy; her happiness is not justified, because she is not actually living up to her own standard. Kraut is committed to denying the happiness of anyone who has false beliefs about her life or lacks a firm connection with reality, so anyone whose happiness is the result of deception, drugs, or virtual reality machines and anyone who is simply misinformed will fail to be happy, regardless of how satisfied she is with her life.

Although Kraut argues that a person can be wrong about her own happiness, he does not believe a person's individual standards are capable of criticism. On Kraut's view, we cannot deny a person's happiness because we view her activities as inappropriate or worthless, or because we believe she values the wrong things. For Kraut, the only way to criticize a person's happiness is on the grounds that she is failing to attain whatever it is that she values. Establishing what is valuable or what standards must be met is left entirely to the subject to decide. Because Kraut allows the subject to determine her own standards of happiness, his account is not vulnerable to the objections raised against the normative theories we considered in the previous section.

There are several contemporary theorists who agree with Kraut's analysis of happiness. They share Kraut's intuition that imposing foreign standards on a person when judging her happiness is inappropriate, yet they explicitly deny that reports of satisfaction are sufficient for happiness. For example, Robert Nozick expresses reluctance at calling someone happy if the judgment that she is happy is based on perceptions that are wildly wrong. "Someone whose emotion is based upon completely and egregiously unjustified and false evaluations we will be reluctant to term happy, however he feels. He should have known better."[18]

Similarly, Wladyslaw Tatarkiewicz defines happiness as lasting, complete, and justified satisfaction with one's life. He adds in the qualification that "it is *justified* satisfaction" to rule out all cases of happiness that are based on illusion or deception.[19] Although such people may be satisfied, according to Tatarkiewicz, we should not call them happy.

John Kekes expresses a view of happiness that very closely mirrors Kraut's, for he believes people are happy when they are satisfied with their lives and their satisfaction is rationally justified. According to Kekes, the standards for happiness are ontologically subjective, but epistemologically objective. They are ontologically subjective because the creation of these standards of happiness is up to the subject and they will reflect her individual values, priorities, and goals. Like Kraut, Kekes does not believe third parties can challenge or criticize the subject's choice of standards. However, the question of whether she is actually succeeding in meeting her standards is an objective matter, meaning it can be judged by any third party and the subject is not in a privileged position to make such a judgment. Kekes explains that once the subject's goals are established, there is an objective fact about whether she is actually attaining whatever it is that she desires, and the subject can be wrong about whether she is meeting her own standards for happiness. Kekes agrees with Kraut that if the subject's satisfaction is not rationally justified by the actual conditions of her life, if she is not meeting her own subjective standards of satisfaction, then she fails to be happy, regardless of how satisfied she may feel.

Finally, Julia Annas agrees that our modern conception of happiness is "extremely flexible in content," meaning it places no restriction on the different standards individuals may use in assessing their own happiness. The modern conception of happiness tolerates quite varied answers to the question of what makes one happy, and we are "willing to allow that just about anything could make her happy."[20] As Annas explains, "Our modern conception of happiness is subjective; if I think I am happy at a given time, then I am."[21] Annas argues that it is the subjectivity of modern theories of happiness that creates the great divide between ancient and modern views. Instead of viewing happiness as arising only from virtuous activity, Annas believes the modern notion allows people latitude in determining what makes them happy, placing no restriction on what can cause a person's happiness.

However, like the other normative theorists we have discussed, Annas does not believe our modern conception of happiness is purely subjective. She argues that it was formed from "a variety of incompatible sources," resulting in a concept of happiness that "contains several different and incompatible elements."[22] Like the other normative theorists, she denies that happiness is simply a matter of being in the right mental state, and she does not believe experiencing satisfaction is sufficient for happiness. To support her claims about happiness, Annas offers the following example. A colleague of hers was teaching a course to business students, and he asked his class about their ideas on when a person is living a happy life. The class cited the typical luxuries often associated with happiness, which included having a big house, cars, and material wealth. The class was then instructed to imagine that a rich relative had died, leaving them all of his money and various luxuries. The class was then asked whether this would make them happy, and the class responded overwhelmingly with the reply, "No."[23]

Annas views this response as indicating that our modern notion of happiness is not merely a matter of getting what you want, "but it also contained the idea of living a certain sort of life, of being active rather than a passive recipient of money and other stuff." She believes our modern view of happiness is intimately connected to the ideas of achievement and activity, and the students' response implies that "my happiness must involve my living a good life." Therefore, she rejects a purely subjective understanding of happiness, because it "leaves out some important and more objective elements which our reflection has uncovered."[24]

Like Kraut and Kekes, Annas is willing to permit the subject latitude in determining what she wishes to achieve. Annas believes every person forms a particular view of the good life based on her own values and priorities, and this enables her to structure her pursuits. For Annas, happiness is necessarily connected with achievement, because being happy implies one is actually achieving her goals. So like Kraut and the other normative theorists, Annas would deny the happiness of anyone whose life fails to warrant the satisfaction she experiences.

Now I shall explain why I believe even this more relaxed version of the normative view of happiness is problematic. My objections will focus mainly on the views of Kraut, Kekes, and Annas, for they provide the most well-defined accounts, but they also apply to all of the normative theorists we have discussed in this section. The plan is to argue that even these more relaxed normative constraints on happiness are too restrictive, leading us to the conclusion that all normative views of happiness should be rejected.

Let us return to the example we discussed earlier involving Jane, the woman who falsely believes that she has a great life, but whose husband is actually having an extramarital affair. Let us suppose that Jane is entirely satisfied with her life and is in no danger of finding out the truth about her husband's affair. The important question is: what should we say about Jane's current state of happiness?

Kraut, along with the other normative theorists, would have to say that Jane is not really happy, because she fails to achieve what she views as constitutive of happiness (namely, a successful marriage). They would view her happiness as unjustified, but I disagree with this analysis. I believe that Jane is happy right now, although she may not be happy if she learns the truth about her husband's antics. To support my contention, imagine that Jane has been killed in a car accident so that she never learns the truth. What would Jane's friends say about her life at her wake? Kraut seems to believe they would say, "Poor Jane, she thought she was so happy, but she really wasn't." But this response sounds wrong, even if her friends knew the truth about her cheating husband. Instead, I believe it is more likely they would say something like, "Poor Jane, she was so happy, but her husband was such a louse. She had no idea."

Consider the way other emotion words function in our language. If I see a shadow and jump in fear and then realize it was nothing, I cannot deny the fear I felt at that moment. Fear is the reason I jumped, even if I am not afraid now because I realize the fear was unjustified. We are emotionally affected by what we believe to be true, even if, in reality, it is false. If someone close to me dies, I cannot feel sad before I am told of the death. Alternatively, if I am told that a dear friend has died, then I will grieve, even if it is a mistake and my friend is alive and well. The same reasoning should apply to happiness: a person's happiness should not be affected by facts she knows nothing about.

Therefore, the emotions a person experiences are directly related to that person's beliefs. As her beliefs change, so too will her level of happiness. But just as it is implausible to expect someone to grieve over a death they know nothing about, it is equally implausible to deny a person's happiness on the basis of facts she knows nothing about. If we are sure that Jane had no suspicions about her husband's affair prior to her death, then we can be confident that her happiness was in no way adversely affected by that truth. This example is reminiscent of the old adage "Ignorance is bliss."

Another problem for the normative theorist is how we are to determine whether someone's happiness is justified. In the case of Jane, the normative theorist would point to the fact that her marriage was a sham and use that fact to deny her happiness. But in many other cases, these "facts" are hardly discernible. Who is to say how well someone is progressing toward her goals and whether that progress is sufficient to warrant her happiness? It seems obvious that the subject herself would be the best-qualified and most relevant judge, yet this option is explicitly rejected by the normative theorist.

In order for the normative theorists' view to be tenable, there must be clear reasons for people's happiness that can be gauged by outside observers, but this is simply not the case in many ordinary situations. For instance, how can their view handle a situation in which the subject is working toward a goal that stretches far into the future, such as raising children or pursuing a doctorate? The subject may be satisfied because she sees herself as slowly working toward this goal. But an outside observer may be doubtful of her progress and instead see her as failing. Who is correct in such cases where there is no obvious deception of the subject, but just a difference of opinion about whether she is "really" meeting her own standard of happiness? According to the normative theorist, a person's happiness is justified only if she is actually achieving her goals, but in many cases, that is impossible to determine right now. So what should we say about such people's happiness? Must we deny it due to a lack of information? Must we say their happiness is indeterminate? If the concept of happiness were this elusive, the word would be rendered nearly useless for practical purposes, and we would never be able to judge whether anyone is happy or unhappy.

Consider one more example. There are some religious people who aim at piety, and the belief that they are achieving this goal makes them very happy. What can the normative theorist say about the happiness of these religious people? If there is no God, these people's happiness is not justified, and they are merely deceived. Must we verify God's existence before we can issue a judgment on their happiness? Furthermore, even if we are willing to grant that God exists, how can we possibly determine whether a person is living piously enough to warrant her happiness? The "goal" in this case is simply too elusive for a third party to use in judging happiness. Unfortunately, none of the normative theorists supply us with a helpful response to these difficulties. Worse still, the normative theorists' view permits the atheist to deny the happiness of the religious person on the grounds that she is deceived. But it also permits the religious person to regard the atheist as deceived and to deny her happiness. Yet in neither case does the judgment of happiness have anything to do with the subject's own mental state. Clearly, this is not the way *happiness* functions in our ordinary language.

Kraut, Kekes, and Annas explicitly recognize the importance of the subject's own values to the question of whether she is happy. For instance, Kraut rejects the idea that we can criticize the standards and goals people adopt, because "we have no defensible method for discovering each person's distance from his ideal lives."[25] I believe the same objection applies to the question of whether a person is meeting her own standards, for it is too difficult to determine how close someone is to realizing her goals. Furthermore, it is not clear why *our* third-party opinion of her progress is even relevant to the question of whether *she* is happy. Therefore, if we are to adopt her standards when judging her happiness, as Kraut urges, then we should also adopt her perspective in judging how well she is reaching those goals.

Let us now turn to the "empirical data" from Annas's example involving the business students, which I shall argue she misinterprets. Rather than indicating something deep about the nature of happiness, I believe we should view the students' response as indicating what would cause satisfaction in them. As a group, they agreed that they would not be satisfied unless they actually worked toward some goal and earned it. However, one cannot argue from one possible source of happiness to the conclusion that this is the only source of happiness, or a description of the nature of happiness itself.

Annas's identification of happiness with personal achievement is especially doubtful when we consider the possibility of someone who accomplishes great things but is never satisfied with her progress. Let us imagine this person is an exceptionally harsh critic of herself and never believes she is doing enough. She constantly dwells on the goals she still has to work toward, and she never steps back to appreciate all of her actual success. Her negativity motivates her to continue to work hard, but given her negative outlook, she is never satisfied. Put simply, she is rarely happy. This example demonstrates why happiness is not necessarily something that you earn or deserve, and being happy says nothing about the value of your life or your accomplishments. You can have a successful life in which you accomplish many great things, but until you can appreciate the value of what you have done, you will never be happy.

Conclusion

The normative theorists we have discussed in this chapter appear to make the same error as the ancient ethicists who equate happiness with virtue: they have taken a word from the average person's lexicon and provided it with a philosophical meaning that has little connection with our everyday concept.[26] I believe part of their motivation for incorporating the additional objective component into happiness comes from the influence of Aristotle, who identified happiness with the greatest good. The normative theorists appear to embrace the Aristotelian thesis that being happy implies that one is living the good life. But if you identify being happy with living a good life, then adopting a life-satisfaction view of happiness would commit you to the idea that you can achieve the good life by doing anything that makes you happy. This is a troubling conclusion when you consider all the potential sources of satisfaction, many of which we would never associate with living "the good life."

The normative theorist clearly wishes to avoid this unsavory conclusion, so she denies that satisfaction is sufficient for happiness, and she incorporates various normative constraints on when a person can be deemed happy. The normative constraints are supposed to ensure that happiness is achieved only by people who partake in the right sorts of meaningful or worthwhile activities, that is, people who are truly living good lives. However, it is the incorporation of these normative constraints that causes these theories to deviate from common usage, thus rendering them objectionable. All normative theorists deny that satisfaction is sufficient for happiness, yet none provides any justification for holding the Aristotelian thesis that conflates happiness with goodness.

I suggest we should reject these theorists' first step and deny the conflation of happiness with the good life. If we separate the realm of happiness from the realms of morality and well-being, we can accept people's happiness without thereby committing ourselves to any particular view of the goodness of their lives. Therefore, we should reject the imposition of all normative constraints on happiness and view statements of happiness not as appraisals or judgments, but as reports that the subject is satisfied with her life. We shall discuss the life-satisfaction view of happiness and what it entails in the next chapter.

Notes

1. John Kekes, "Happiness," in *The Encyclopedia of Ethics,* edited by L. C. Becker and C. B. Becker (New York: Garland, 1992), 644–650.

2. Richard Kraut, "Two Conceptions of Happiness," *Philosophical Review* 88 (1979): 170.

3. Jean Austin, "Pleasure and Happiness," *Philosophy* 43 (1968): 53.

4. R. M. Hare, *Freedom and Reason* (Oxford: Oxford University Press, 1969), 126.

5. Ibid.

6. Ibid., 127.

7. Ibid., 128.

8. J. J. C. Smart, "An Outline of a System of Utilitarian Ethics," in *Utilitarianism: For and Against,* edited by J. J. C. Smart and Bernard Williams (New York: Cambridge University Press, 1973), 22.

9. Ibid., 22–23.

10. Robert Simpson, "Happiness," *American Philosophical Quarterly* 12 (1975): 173.

11. Lynne McFall, *Happiness* (New York: Peter Lang, 1982), 18, 35, 93.

12. Ibid., 35.

13. Ibid., 126.

14. Deal W. Hudson, *Happiness and the Limits of Satisfaction* (Lanham, MD: Rowman and Littlefield, 1996), 116.

15. Kraut, "Two Conceptions of Happiness," 178.

16. Ibid., 179, 180.

17. Ibid., 179.

18. Robert Nozick, *The Examined Life* (New York: Simon and Schuster, 1989), 111.

19. Wladyslaw Tatarkiewicz, *Analysis of Happiness,* Melbourne International Philosophy Series, vol. 3 (Warsaw: Polish Scientific Publishers, 1976), 13.

20. Julia Annas, "Should Virtue Make You Happy?," *Aepiron* 35 (2003): 13.

21. Julia Annas, "Virtue and Eudaimonism," *Social Philosophy and Policy* 15 (1998): 51.

22. Ibid., 53–54.

23. Annas, "Should Virtue Make You Happy?," 18–19.

24. Ibid., 19.

25. Kraut, "Two Conceptions of Happiness," 192.

26. I should note that thinkers in a range of disciplines are revisiting these ancient ideas about happiness, and the latest scientific research validates at least some of what the ancients believed about how many people achieve happiness. Unfortunately, this issue lies beyond the scope of this book, but see Sissela Bok's recent book *Exploring Happiness* (New Haven, CT: Yale University Press, 2010), where she brings together current empirical research and historical ideas about happiness. See also psychologist Jonathan Haidt's book *The Happiness Hypothesis* (New York: Basic Books, 2005).

CHAPTER SIX

Happiness as Life Satisfaction

We are now left with one more theory of happiness to consider, the life-satisfaction view, which I shall argue presents us with the best account of the nature and value of happiness. The goal of this chapter is to reach a definition of happiness that is theoretically useful, because it enables us to characterize people's motives and behavior, but also accords well with common usage. Thus far, we have critically evaluated many popular theories of happiness and found them to be objectionable, mainly because they violated our commonsense intuitions about happiness. We shall continue to rely on those intuitions in evaluating the life-satisfaction view, which essentially reduces happiness to a person's satisfaction with her life. The life-satisfaction view improves upon the theories we rejected in the previous chapter, because it does not place any normative constraints on how a person achieves happiness. As long as a person is satisfied, she will be happy, regardless of the cause of her satisfaction.

This chapter begins by examining the different versions of the life-satisfaction view from the contemporary literature. I discuss what these views share in common and address several misconceptions about happiness. In the next two sections, I consider the question of whether there are different concepts of happiness and whether it makes sense to say that we can be mistaken about our own happiness. In the final section, I reply to an objection, which charges that happiness cannot be reduced to life satisfaction because life satisfaction is arbitrary. I argue that this objection rests on a misunderstanding of what being satisfied entails, and I conclude that the life-satisfaction view still provides us with the most plausible theory of happiness that best represents the way we use the word today.

The Life-Satisfaction View

The life-satisfaction view of happiness has enjoyed considerable popularity among both philosophers and psychologists. Put simply, this view says that a person is happy to the extent that she is satisfied with her life, and the more favorable her impression, the happier she will be. However, a brief glance at the literature suggests there are many different interpretations of this view. For instance, Theodore Benditt describes a person as happy if she is disposed, when she considers her life, to feel satisfied, which means she judges that her expectations are being attained. Richard Brandt argues that in order to be happy, it is necessary that one like those parts of one's total life pattern and circumstances that one thinks are important. Robin Barrow identifies happiness with having a favorable attitude toward whatever relationship one happens to have to one's circumstances, and Elizabeth Telfer defines happiness as a state of being pleased with your life as a whole.[1]

One feature shared by all life-satisfaction views is the idea that the happy person has a favorable impression, attitude, or perception of her life. All life-satisfaction theorists agree that liking your life or viewing it positively is necessary for happiness. It follows that someone who is unhappy can become happy by either changing her circumstances or changing her attitude toward her life (perhaps by changing her standards, expectations, or values). This highlights the importance of expectation to an individual's happiness.

Life-satisfaction views also recognize the importance of experiencing positive feelings, for happiness is incompatible with negative emotional states, such as anxiety, disappointment, and depression. As Brandt notes, "If a man is happy, he will not be subject . . . to gloom, anxiety, restlessness, depression, discouragement, and shame, for these feelings will not occur if he likes the total pattern of his life insofar as the parts he deems important are concerned." Similarly, Barrow believes that "happy people . . . are those who do not suffer from things such as despair, dismay, alienation, loneliness, frustration or disappointment; they are content with the world as they perceive it and with their lot in it."[2]

Happiness is a degree concept, which refers to feelings that range in intensity from mild contentment to extreme joy. One does not have to experience feelings of glee or ecstasy in order to be happy. For some, happiness may involve only the experience of modest satisfaction or contentment. But all happy people experience some positive feelings, because they are satisfied with their lives, and a person's happiness will be proportional to how positively she views her life.

Being satisfied with something implies that the subject's hopes, expectations, and demands are involved. According to Benditt, "If a man says that he is satisfied with his accomplishments, he implies that what he has accomplished does not (significantly) fall short of his hopes and expectations, with the goals which he has, explicitly or implicitly, set for himself." However, one can be satisfied with something without being satisfied with every aspect of that thing. As Benditt notes, "One need only be satisfied with most of it, or with the important aspects of it, so that on the whole one's satisfaction with something sufficiently outweighs the dissatisfaction with it."[3] Applying this reasoning to happiness, we can see that one may be happy with her life overall without being completely happy about every aspect thereof. For instance, I may be happy with my life, even if I am currently having some problems at work or with a family member, as long as the positive aspects outweigh the negative.

Life-satisfaction theories differ in their descriptions of satisfaction, for some describe it in terms of making a judgment or appraisal of one's life, while others describe satisfaction in more emotional terms.[4] For example, G. H. Von Wright views happiness as liking your circumstances in life. "Happiness *is* not in the circumstances . . . but springs into being with the relationship. . . . To judge oneself happy is to pass judgment on or value one's circumstances of life." Brandt views one person as happier than another "if he likes a larger proportion of the aspects of his life pattern or circumstances that he deems important, or if he likes them better than the other person." Similarly, L. W. Sumner believes happiness consists in a positive evaluation of the conditions of your life, which is a judgment that it measures up favorably against your standards or expectations.[5]

In contrast, Telfer presents a more emotional understanding of satisfaction, for she identifies happiness as an "attitude of mind" that implies one is pleased with her life as a whole, where being pleased simply means that one wants to have it as it is. According to Telfer, the happy person "does not want anything major in his life to be otherwise; he is pleased with . . . what he has got; [and] there is nothing major which he has not got and which he wants." Similarly, Barrow describes happiness in terms of having a sense of enmeshment with one's world, which involves seeing the world as one would like it to be. Barrow argues that happiness involves judgment only in the most minimal sense of categorizing one's feelings (for example, as being happy as opposed to miserable), but he denies that they involve appraisal in the sense of assessment of the conditions in which one finds oneself. According to Barrow, in order to state that I am happy, I do not need to examine my circumstances and check that they meet certain criteria; being happy can be settled simply by introspecting one's own state of mind.[6]

I am inclined to favor the more emotional understanding of satisfaction, for I see no reason to specify the cause of a person's happiness or limit it to a judgment or appraisal. The important point embraced by all life-satisfaction theorists is the idea that happiness is a state of satisfaction, and it should not matter how one achieves that state. Although the happiness of many (perhaps even most) people may arise from judgments about their lives, positive perceptions can also be caused by taking the right drugs, plugging into a virtual reality machine, or engaging in self-deception. In this regard, happiness can be compared to depression, for different people can be depressed for different reasons, and to different degrees, yet all are classified as depressed. Similarly, all happy people share a positive attitude toward life, although that attitude may differ in both its cause and its intensity.

Although saying that two people are happy implies they share the same state of mind, the degree to which they feel happy may differ, just as the happiness experienced by the same person on different occasions may differ. Some people never get too high or too low, preferring to keep all emotional reactions under control. Others swing wildly between happiness and unhappiness, experiencing joy and sorrow with each new event that occurs. Upon falling in love with someone new, a person may experience a kind of happiness she never knew before. As Barrow explains, "The happiness that you and I experience may be different in texture, or experientially, while nonetheless being happiness in exactly the same sense, just as the beauty of one woman may differ from that of another, while being no more and no less an instance of beauty in the same sense of the word."[7]

Happiness is best characterized as a mental state of the subject, not as a state of affairs occurring in the world, and there are no necessary material conditions of happiness. We can describe someone without contradiction as "poor, but happy," "wicked, but happy," or even "alone, but happy." If the subject has a favorable impression of her life and reports her happiness, there is no way for an outside observer to dispute her claim. As Sumner explains, "Happiness (or unhappiness) is a response by a subject to her life conditions *as she sees them*. It is a matter of whether she is finding the *perceived* conditions of her life satisfying or fulfilling."[8] There are, however, certain states of mind that are incompatible with happiness, for one cannot be "depressed, but happy," "lonely, but happy," or "frustrated, but happy."[9] All of these states imply that the subject has certain negative feelings about her life that she would not have if she were happy.

Therefore, the statement "I am happy" will be false under only two conditions: when the subject is lying or when she does not possess the concept *happiness*. In either case, a third party would be justified in denying the report of happiness. Under all other circumstances, the subject's sincere report of happiness will be sufficient for her being happy. Reports of happiness are similar to pain reports in this respect; if the subject honestly claims to be in pain, and she knows what this word means, she cannot be proven wrong by a third party. Or consider a parallel example with hunger: suppose you tell someone that you are hungry, and their response is that you must be mistaken, because you've already had enough to eat. This reply is inappropriate because third parties cannot usually defeat claims about your own mental or physical state. The same reasoning applies to happiness: third-party opinions about whether your life warrants satisfaction are irrelevant to the question of whether you are happy with your life.

Barrow accepts both of these conditions, but he adds a third way for first-person judgments about happiness to be mistaken, which is when the subject is guilty of making a faulty comparison. According to Barrow, such cases occur because "I may claim to be happy when such a claim is *inconsistent* with my normal standards for judging myself to be happy, or I may claim to be happy now, but subsequently come to appreciate that what I then experienced was so much less in degree than I am capable of that it should not have counted as happiness."[10]

I am not convinced that we should accept Barrow's third condition. On Barrow's view, someone would be guilty of making a faulty comparison when her new experience of happiness is so radically different from her old experience that it is supposed to cause her to doubt her past reports of happiness. But happiness is a degree concept, which means it refers to a range of states that vary greatly in their felt intensity. If all of the subject's past experiences of happiness were at the lower end of this spectrum, she may not have realized how intense happiness can be. The subject's new experience will teach her something about her past experiences—namely, that they were not very happy—but it should not cause her to doubt her past satisfaction. Rather, she can now appreciate the full range of experiences to which this word refers.

Consider a parallel example with depression. Sally has experienced depression several times in her life, but one day something horrific happens that causes her to go into a deep depression that is much worse than anything she has ever experienced. This new experience may open Sally's eyes up to how bad depression can be. Barrow's view implies that Sally's present experience could cause her to doubt whether she has ever experienced depression before. But this analysis misdescribes the case, for Sally did experience sadness and pain in the past. Instead, we should say that Sally's understanding of depression is broadened by her new experience, and now she better appreciates the range of states to which this term refers. There is no need for Sally to retract her past reports of depression, for there is nothing wrong with those reports. She was previously depressed, only to a much less degree than she is now. The same reasoning applies to happiness. Having a new, more intense experience will not falsify your past reports of happiness; it only broadens your understanding of how good or intense that emotion can be. Therefore, Barrow's posit of an additional way to be wrong about your own happiness is unnecessary.

John Rawls's version of the life-satisfaction view identifies happiness as arising from the successful execution of one's rational life plan. According to Rawls, "Someone is happy when his plans are going well, his more important aspirations are being fulfilled, and he feels sure that his good fortune will endure." Given the diversity of people's natural abilities and life circumstances, Rawls acknowledges the potential diversity in what plans people will choose to adopt. Rawls argues that "being happy involves both a certain achievement in action and a rational assurance about the outcome."[11]

I agree with Rawls that being happy for some people is a function of moving toward their goals, but I wonder whether it applies to everyone. I believe it is also possible for someone to be happy in the absence of such clearly defined goals, as in the person who simply drifts through life. So long as the drifter is satisfied with her life, the mere absence of a well-defined plan should not automatically prevent her from being happy. Rawls acknowledges the possibility of the drifter, and he attempts to explain this case by arguing, "The limit decision to have no plan at all, to let things come as they may, is still theoretically a plan that may or may not be rational."[12] However, it is unclear how Rawls's account can recognize the happiness of the drifter, when he uses the proportion of the subject's aims that are being achieved to determine a person's happiness. The drifter lacks such goals, and therefore lacks a necessary condition of happiness, according to Rawls.

Rawls mistakenly places the emphasis on the successful pursuit of one's goals, instead of on the subject's state of satisfaction, which may be completely unrelated to her achievements. It may be true that for many people, experiencing satisfaction will be intimately connected with achieving one's aims, but as Roger Montague notes, "there are unreflective people who do not even realize that their priorities are muddled, and others who muddle cheerfully."[13] We have no reason to presume these people, just like our drifter, cannot be happy.

Rawls's use of *rationality* in his characterization of happiness is also problematic. Consider the person who truthfully says that she is happy staring at a blank wall, day after day (an activity I assume it is not rational to pursue). We have no reason to deny her happiness, presuming she issues an honest report and knows what the word *happy* means. Rawls must deny her happiness, given the irrationality of her pursuit, but this assessment seems incorrect. As outside observers, we may not be able to understand how anyone could be happy under such circumstances, but our opinions about how the wall starer chooses to spend her time have no bearing on the question of her happiness. If she is satisfied with her life, there does not appear to be anything from a conceptual standpoint that prevents her from being happy.

A further problem for Rawls is that imposing rational constraints on the causes of a person's happiness may result in a slippery slope. For example, if you can deny the happiness of "the wall starer," you open the door for someone else to deny the happiness of the accountant (who stares at people's tax returns all day) on the grounds that his career choice is so dull, no one could possibly find such a job satisfying. Perhaps he likes his job, just as the wall starer, because of a rare brain abnormality, likes staring at walls. This suggests third-party opinions about how people choose to spend their time are totally irrelevant to the question of happiness.

Is There One Concept of Happiness?

One question that is frequently discussed within the literature is whether there are distinct concepts of happiness or simply one concept that can be used in different ways. Several theorists writing about happiness accept the former claim, including D. A. Lloyd Thomas, who argues that *happiness* stands for a group of related concepts. Similarly, Wladyslaw Tatarkiewicz and Lynne McFall describe happiness as having distinct meanings or senses, while Sumner, Telfer, and Nozick speak of different types, kinds, or dimensions of happiness.[14]

The following four categories represent the most frequently discussed "uses" or "senses" of happiness found within the literature: (1) being happy with or about something, (2) feeling happy, (3) having a happy disposition or personality, and (4) being happy or having a happy life.[15] Obviously, this list is not exhaustive of *all* of the possible uses of *happiness,* which appears in countless collocations and phrases, including *happy couple, happy ending, happy accident,* and *happy hour,* to name just a few. Rather than discuss every possible use of *happiness,* which would be of little philosophical interest, I shall limit my discussion to the four main categories listed above to see if they do in fact represent distinct concepts with different meanings or senses. I shall argue that there is only one concept of happiness with one meaning that is simply applied in different contexts. Happiness refers to a state of satisfaction in the subject, regardless of whether that state is caused by some particular event (happy with or about) or from the contemplation of one's life (being happy or having a happy life) or is used to describe someone's general mood (happy disposition or personality). But in all four cases, it is the same state that is being targeted.

Let us begin with (1), being happy with or about something. This is clearly an instance of the fourth use, being happy. The only relevant difference is that (4) has a wider scope and is applied to a person's life as a whole, but they both still refer to the same state of satisfaction. For example, "being happy with your job" implies that you view it positively and that it meets (or exceeds) your expectations. "Being happy" means exactly the same thing, only you are referring more broadly to your life overall. Therefore, we need not draw a distinction between (1) and (4), because there is just one concept that is being used in two different ways.

The same reasoning applies to (3), having a happy disposition or personality. Telfer describes a happy temperament as "a disposition to be cheerful, to find things agreeable," which "suits its wishes to the circumstances more readily than average."[16] Having a happy disposition or personality implies that one is more likely to be satisfied and less likely to be dissatisfied when compared with the average person. One reason a person is more likely to experience satisfaction is because she has flexible, undemanding standards, which are easily met. But the less one demands from life, and the lower one's expectations, the easier it will be for one to achieve satisfaction. On the other hand, the more you expect, the harder it will be to achieve happiness. So the person with a happy disposition may simply be predisposed to having low expectations or standards, thus making it easier for her to achieve satisfaction with her life.

People with happy dispositions may also be predisposed to having strong coping mechanisms, which enable them to handle adversities well. These people may be able to maintain a consistent state of satisfaction or cheerfulness, because they refuse to let any recalcitrant events bring them down. This insight is perhaps best articulated by the Stoics, who identify happiness with living a life of virtue, which amounts to resigning oneself to whatever external events occur and adopting an attitude of apathy or indifference to them. If you refuse to let any external events affect your emotional state, then you will be able to maintain a consistent level of satisfaction regardless of what you face in life, and this is the same as saying that you have a happy disposition or personality. Therefore, having a happy disposition or personality is just another instance of (4), being happy or having a happy life.

Finally, let us consider the distinction between (4), being happy, and (2), feeling happy. Feeling happy is described as "a (temporary) inclination to look on the bright side or find things agreeable," which is often explained in terms of being in a happy mood.[17] Telfer argues that the distinction between feeling and being happy is more than just one of degree, for they actually differ in kind. I believe it is a mistake to draw a distinction between being happy and feeling happy, because *happiness* functions similarly to other emotion words. For example, does it make sense to say that you feel scared, but then to deny that you are actually scared? Similarly, can you say that you only feel angry, but that you aren't actually angry? Neither claim makes much sense, because "feeling" any of these emotions implies that one is experiencing them. If one "feels pain," then one is in pain, and if one "feels sad," then one is sad; there is no principled way to separate the "feeling" from the "being." The same is true of happiness, and if one "feels happy," then one is happy.

Furthermore, from a phenomenological perspective, how could we tell the difference between feeling and being happy? You say, "I feel *happy*," as opposed to feeling some other emotion, because you feel the way you normally do when you *are* happy. If there were a noticeable difference in the feeling itself, you would not refer to your state as "happiness," but you would call it something else instead. Even Sumner, who accepts the distinction between being and feeling happy, recognizes this point. He says that feelings of happiness are generally short-lived; however, "they are capable (at least in principle) of enduring for some time, at which point they become difficult to distinguish from a settled sense of satisfaction with the conditions of one's life."[18] But in that case, feeling happy is just being happy, and it is not clear why we should draw a distinction between the two.

Since feeling and being happy are indistinguishable from inside the subject, the only way one could differentiate between them would be from the outside. But this would imply there is a normative standard to which we could appeal in order to judge whether someone is "really" happy or merely "feels happy." But we have already shown that the imposition of such standards is unjustified, because happiness refers to the subject's state of satisfaction regardless of how she achieves that satisfaction. In the absence of such standards, however, there is no principled way to differentiate between feeling and being happy. Therefore, if a subject feels happy, she is happy, for her mental state is the same in both cases.

To recap, I have shown that (1) being happy with or about something and (3) having a happy disposition or personality are really just instances of (4) being happy or having a happy life. I have also shown that there is no difference between (2) feeling happy and (4) being happy or having a happy life. Since all of these distinct uses of *happiness* employ exactly the same concept, drawing a distinction between them is unnecessary. Once you have a proper under-standing of happiness as being in a state of satisfaction with your life, the question of how to apply the word to these different contexts is clear.

Are Mistakes About Happiness Possible?

The next issue is whether the subject can be wrong about her own happiness. We have already touched upon this question in connection with the normative theories of happiness we discussed in Chapter 5, which sought to impose external standards on happiness judgments. Although we found the use of such standards to be unfounded, because the subject has first-person authority over her own happiness, in this section I want to focus on the question of whether a person can be mistaken about her own happiness.

Both John Kekes and Richard Kraut agree that happiness involves being in a state of satisfaction, which is related to getting or doing the important things that one wants. A person experiences satisfaction with her life when she determines that enough of her important wants are being met. Whether a particular want is important will depend on one's life plan, which Kekes describes as a hierarchical ordering of one's priorities that ultimately reflects her long-term goals and aspirations. A person will be happy when she realizes her life plan, meaning she is living up to her own individually determined standards of happiness. According to Kekes and Kraut, the possibility of error in happiness judgments arises because the subject can be wrong about whether she is actually living up to her own standards. Put simply, both theorists believe the subject can be shown to be mistaken on her own terms.

Although I agree with Kekes and Kraut about the subject determining her own standards of happiness, I disagree with them about the possibility of error in happiness judgments. I believe we should not allow an outside observer to deny the happiness of a person who truthfully asserts that she is happy and behaves accordingly, and I shall discuss several problems with the view that people can be mistaken about their own happiness.

Kekes and Kraut typically rely on examples of deception in order to illustrate how people's truthful reports of happiness can be mistaken. In these cases, a person's entire reason for being happy is based on a lie, and both theorists agree that gives us reason to deny a person's happiness, even if this person is completely ignorant of the truth. I believe the more natural interpretation is that the deceived person will become unhappy when she learns the truth, but this cannot change the fact that she is happy prior to being told. As Barrow explains, "A building is no less a building because it is built on insecure foundations, although it may not remain one for very long."[19]

One problem for Kekes and Kraut is how to conceptualize a person's life plan, such that it can be used as a litmus test for gauging whether she is actually achieving happiness or is only under the false impression that she is happy. The subject's belief that she is satisfied with her life is supposed to be fallible, because we can show her that she is wrong "on her own terms." Presumably, this error is made clear to the subject by referring to her life plan. But most people do not possess anything like the highly structured life plans that Kekes envisions, and the "plans" many people have for ordering their goals or desires are not sufficiently well defined to provide such a test. Although people survey their lives, many do not consciously take note of the progress and regress of each and every relevant factor, nor are they even conscious of which specific factors combine to form their overall perceptions of their lives. Most people do have a general sense of how things in their lives are going; however, their impressions, especially when things are fine, may involve nothing more than a positive or negative feeling.

Furthermore, to carry out such a detailed analysis would be not only time-consuming, but also a wasteful exercise, because our lives are constantly changing. Which desires are the "most important" will be subject to change, depending on a person's experiences and on the context. The notion of a life plan providing a fixed ordering for one's desires misrepresents the actual state of most people's desires, which are better described as being in flux. But in the absence of a static life plan, it is not clear what grounds a third-party observer could appeal to in order to convince the subject that she is not really happy. Even if we are willing to grant that a third party may criticize the subject's pursuits or offer the subject advice, the subject need not accept the advice or embrace the criticism.

Furthermore, even in those cases where people have sufficiently well-structured life plans, realizing them (or failing to realize them) still may have no connection with happiness. Consider the following scenario. Susie is a graduate student who is currently working on her dissertation. She is quite satisfied with her progress thus far, and she hopes to complete her thesis soon. One day Susie has a meeting with another professor in her department, and he asks her how she is doing. She explains that she is happy, and she proceeds to list precisely why she is satisfied with her progress. She details what she has already accomplished and how she plans to achieve the rest of her goals, which include securing a tenure-track job at a reputable university. Let us suppose this professor does not have an equally positive impression of Susie's progress or her prospects for reaching her goals. He tells her that he does not approve of her choice of topic or adviser. He also tells her that she has overlooked certain factors critical to achieving her goals, such as having teaching experience, presenting papers at professional conferences, and getting her work published.

We can assume that Susie was happy with her life before speaking with this professor: she viewed her progress positively and had high hopes for the future. But as a result of this conversation, Susie's view of her life has changed. She now sees her progress, her topic, and even her adviser differently, and she is no longer satisfied with any of them. Susie's happiness may slowly recede, or it may disappear altogether as the stark realization sets in that she has been deluding herself. She now believes she has a more realistic understanding of her life and her prospects for the future. Although she is now unhappy, she is grateful for the enlightenment, for she can now begin to initiate changes that will help her to actually achieve her goals.

The crucial question is whether it makes sense to say that Susie was unhappy all along, even before speaking with the professor, because she was previously deceived about whether she was accomplishing her goals. Clearly, she thought she was happy, but was she mistaken? Does the "fact" that her happiness was based on a misperception suggest that we should deny that Susie was ever happy? I do not believe that it does, for if you spoke with Susie previously, she would have provided you with a long list of valid reasons for why she believed that she was happy. Although she no longer regards those reasons as important, the old reasons were relevant at the time, and they provided justification for her happiness. I do not see why we should deny Susie's previous state of happiness simply because she has changed her view of her life. Clearly, all of her past beliefs and behavior indicated that she was happy. While under the false impression, Susie appeared content and satisfied, and she had no desire to make significant changes in her life. She did not exhibit any of the behavior of a person who was not happy. In contrast, Susie's current behavior does suggest that she is unhappy, for she is initiating changes in order to alleviate the dissatisfaction she now feels.

Consider another example for further illustration. Tom walks into an ice cream shop and orders a vanilla cone. Someone says to him, "You know, there are a lot of other flavors, besides vanilla." Tom may be inspired by this comment to try something new, and upon experiencing the wonders of Rocky Road and Jamoca Almond Fudge, he begins to view plain old vanilla differently. He may find that he no longer enjoys its pure simplicity, and when he does eat vanilla ice cream, he finds himself longing for more complex and sophisticated flavors. Tom's tastes have changed, and it is clear that he is no longer satisfied with his old favorite, vanilla.

Should we say that Tom was never happy eating vanilla ice cream because it did not meet his gastronomical standards? Should we say that Tom only thought that he was enjoying his ice cream prior to his experience of other flavors, but that he was actually mistaken? Clearly, this would not be appropriate. We generally make assumptions about a person's mental state based on her behavior, and how someone behaves usually provides a good indication of what she is thinking and feeling. When the unenlightened Tom ordered vanilla ice cream, he did so because he liked the taste of vanilla and eating it made him happy. Although he has since changed his standards, the fact that it satisfied him in the past seems unquestionable. Why else would he have continued to order it? As with Susie's case, I see no plausible reason to deny Tom's past happiness.

To fully appreciate the implications of believing people can be mistaken about their own happiness, consider one more example, but this time it involves a case of unhappiness. Let us imagine a student walks into the dean's office to voice her dissatisfaction with the university. The dean replies to her complaint by saying, "This school has *everything* you wanted, and it clearly meets all of your standards. Therefore, you cannot be unhappy here—it's impossible! You must be happy, but you just don't realize it!" Clearly, the dean's denial of the student's unhappiness is highly inappropriate and does nothing to make her feel better. The student knows how she feels, and the dean's insistence that she is wrong is actually insulting. I believe it is equally improper to say that people can be mistaken about their own happiness.

Is Life Satisfaction Arbitrary?

Daniel Haybron argues that happiness cannot be reduced to being satisfied with one's life, because we lack stable, well-defined attitudes toward our lives. Haybron believes the life-satisfaction view is committed to three assumptions: first, people have certain attitudes toward their lives; second, these attitudes are well grounded in what they take to be the important facts about their lives; and third, these attitudes are fairly stable, varying mainly with changes in how individuals' lives are going.[20] The problem, according to Haybron, is that a consideration of various empirical studies suggests these assumptions are false, and, therefore, we have a serious reason to doubt the plausibility of the life-satisfaction view of happiness.

The first question is whether the life-satisfaction view is actually committed to all three assumptions, which I believe it is not. Although the life-satisfaction view does require a person to have a positive attitude toward her life, it does not specify the causal origin of that state of satisfaction and, therefore, does not require the positive attitude to be stable or "well-grounded in important facts" about one's life. One can be pleased with her life, even if she is utterly confused about the actual conditions of her life and even if she has intentionally taken drugs that make her deluded about the actual conditions of her life. As long as the subject views her life positively, she will be happy, regardless of how she reaches that state.

Haybron's objection to the life-satisfaction view relies on several studies done by psychologists that show subjects' self-reports of happiness to be highly influenced by context. For example, contextual factors such as being given a candy bar before questioning, being in an unpleasant testing room, and being in the presence of a handicapped person have been shown to have some influence on how subjects judge the quality of their lives as a whole. The subject's mood and the weather (being tested on a sunny versus a rainy day) were also shown to exert some influence on their self-reports. According to Haybron, some psychologists interpret this data as suggesting our reports of life satisfaction "are not reports of previously established attitudes but reflect, rather, *judgments* made at the time of questioning. These judgments are 'best considered constructions in response to particular questions posed at a particular time.' Most often . . . we consider how we feel at the moment and base our judgment on that."[21]

But these empirical data are not conclusive, for psychologists disagree about the severity of the effect of context on subjects' self-reports. Subsequent studies have shown that "transient factors play a smaller role in life satisfaction reports" and that "information about important life domains (like family) plays a larger role." Haybron even admits that "context sensitivities may well wash out over large groups of individuals" and that "self-reports correlate somewhat strongly with other relevant quantities such as reports of affect—and significantly, life satisfaction reports correlate strongly with reported satisfaction with specific domains that people tend to consider important." He adds that life-satisfaction reports "appear to be substantially grounded in important facts, or at least to correlate well with them."[22] This suggests an alternative reading of the empirical data, which actually support the life-satisfaction view of happiness. Rather than assume we lack these attitudes altogether, we can say that people do have the requisite attitudes toward their lives, but these attitudes are simply being influenced by the researchers' manipulation of context.

Let's take a closer look at the empirical studies Haybron cites to see whether they contradict the life-satisfaction view of happiness. Researchers have found that several contextual factors influence people's judgments of life satisfaction, including the order of the questions posed. For example, asking people first about their marriages and then about their satisfaction with their lives generates a different response than when the questions are reversed. Subjects were also asked to recall positive or negative events from the past, and these too were found to exert some influence on their subsequent judgments of satisfaction.[23]

One explanation for these phenomena is that the information contained in prior questions influenced the subject's perception of her life and her judgments of satisfaction. For example, asking about past traumas and triumphs brings that information to the forefront of the subject's memory. She may not have even thought of this past event in issuing her judgment of satisfaction, had the researchers not primed her with the prior questioning. The researchers conclude that the subjects' judgments of life satisfaction "crucially depend on the information that is accessible at the time of judgment and how this information is used in constructing mental representations of the to-be-evaluated episode and a relevant standard."[24] But none of these data disproves the life-satisfaction view of happiness, which predicts that people will issue judgments about their lives based on their perceptions. Clearly, those perceptions will be influenced by various factors, including what information is brought to the attention of the subject at that time. Regardless of how people arrive at their judgments of satisfaction, it is still the subject's perception of her life that determines her level of happiness.

Furthermore, in a study not discussed by Haybron, researchers asked respondents to report on their happiness as well as their satisfaction with their lives. When these two questions were asked on different questionnaires, both reports showed a high correlation. That is, the respondents' mean happiness ratings did not differ from their mean satisfaction ratings, "suggesting that they did not differentiate between these concepts."[25] This finding suggests the average person identifies happiness with satisfaction, thus lending further support for the life-satisfaction view of happiness.

The empirical research also probes the influence of mood on people's judgments of satisfaction. In several different experiments, researchers found reports of satisfaction were influenced by factors like finding a dime on a copy machine, spending time in a pleasant rather than unpleasant room, or watching the German soccer team win rather than lose a championship game.[26] Even the weather was found to have some influence on people's judgments about their lives: respondents reported being in a better mood and being happier on sunny rather than on rainy days.

But the life-satisfaction theorist can readily acknowledge the influence of mood on judgments of satisfaction. As the researchers explain, "Individuals in a happy mood are more likely to recall positive information from memory, whereas individuals in a sad mood are more likely to recall negative information. Hence, thinking about one's life while in a good mood may result in a selective retrieval of positive aspects of one's life, and therefore in a more positive evaluation."[27] Once again, it is the subject's perception of her life that is the determinant of whether she is happy.

Interestingly, the noted effect of weather on subjects' reports of satisfaction was eliminated when the subjects' attention was subtly drawn to the weather as a possible cause of their current feelings. "Under this condition, respondents interviewed on rainy days reported being as happy and satisfied as respondents interviewed on sunny days."[28] By drawing the subjects' attention to the possible influence of the weather, the subjects were able to consciously disregard this factor as irrelevant, thereby eliminating its possible influence.

Therefore, a person's satisfaction with her life will be a function of how well she perceives herself as measuring up in the areas she deems important. The empirical studies indicate a person's perception can be influenced by context, but I question the significance of this influence, since its effects can be eliminated completely, as is demonstrated by the study involving the weather. In some cases, the influence of contextual factors is better compared to background noise, as opposed to providing real insight into a person's satisfaction or happiness.

The following example can help to illustrate this point. Suppose that you are eating a meal in a nice restaurant. Your experience will be influenced by countless factors, including the ambience, your mental and physical states (including mood and hunger), the quality of the food, and the price. If you are asked to evaluate your satisfaction with your meal on a particular occasion, you might attempt to block out all of those factors not directly related to the quality of the food itself in order to issue a fair appraisal. But imagine there is a screaming baby at the very next table. Although you may try to focus on the food presentation and the taste, your judgment of satisfaction with the meal will probably be negatively impacted by the screaming baby, perhaps to the extent that it prevents you from enjoying your meal altogether.

The same sort of effect occurs when the researcher manipulates the experimental conditions to elicit a change in the subject's perceived quality of life. The subject isn't actually any more or less satisfied with her life, but as in the case of the restaurant, she is being distracted by irrelevant background noise. Just as the screaming child had little to do with the person's satisfaction with her meal, the influence of context over a person's judgment of satisfaction with her life has little to do with that person's happiness. Therefore, the empirical data do not support Haybron's objection, and judgments of life satisfaction are far from arbitrary.

In the next chapter, we shall investigate the question of whether there is a connection between happiness and morality.

Notes

1. Theodore Benditt, "Happiness," *Philosophical Studies* 25 (1974): 8; Richard Brandt, "Happiness," in *The Encyclopedia of Philosophy,* edited by P. Edwards (New York: Macmillan, 1967), 413; Robin Barrow, *Happiness and Schooling* (New York: St. Martin's Press, 1982), 73; Elizabeth Telfer, *Happiness* (New York: St. Martin's Press, 1980), 8.

2. Brandt, "Happiness," 413; Robin Barrow, *Utilitarianism* (Brookfield, VT: Edward Elgar, 1991), 41.

3. Benditt, "Happiness," 8, 9.

4. For more on the differences between life-satisfaction views of happiness, see Fred Feldman, *What Is This Thing Called Happiness?* (New York: Oxford University Press, 2010), chap. 5.

5. Georg Henrik Von Wright, *The Varieties of Goodness* (Bristol, England: Thoemmes Press, 1996), 98; Brandt, "Happiness," 414; L. W. Sumner, *Welfare, Happiness, and Ethics* (New York: Oxford University Press, 1999), 145.

6. Telfer, *Happiness,* 5–9; Barrow, *Happiness and Schooling,* 74–77.

7. Ibid., 69.

8. Sumner, *Welfare, Happiness, and Ethics,* 156.

9. Jean Austin, "Pleasure and Happiness," *Philosophy* 43 (1968): 60–62.

10. Barrow, *Happiness and Schooling,* 84.

11. John Rawls, *A Theory of Justice* (Cambridge, MA: Harvard University Press, 1971), 480, 481.

12. Ibid., 363.

13. Roger Montague, "Happiness," *Proceedings of the Aristotelian Society* 67 (1967): 89.

14. D. A. Lloyd Thomas, "Happiness," *Philosophical Quarterly* 17 (1968): 97–113; Wladyslaw Tatarkiewicz, *Analysis of Happiness,* Melbourne International Philosophy Series, vol. 3 (Warsaw: Polish Scientific Publishers, 1976), chap. 1; Lynne McFall, *Happiness* (New York: Peter Lang, 1982), chap. 2; Sumner, *Welfare, Happiness, and Ethics,* 143; Telfer, *Happiness,* chap. 1; Robert Nozick, *The Examined Life* (New York: Simon and Schuster, 1989), chap. 10.

15. Sumner, *Welfare, Happiness, and Ethics,* 143.

16. Telfer, *Happiness,* 1, 11.

17. Ibid. See also Sumner, *Welfare, Happiness, and Ethics,* 144.

18. Sumner, *Welfare, Happiness, and Ethics,* 147.

19. Barrow, *Happiness and Schooling,* 84.

20. Daniel Haybron, *The Pursuit of Unhappiness* (New York: Oxford University Press, 2008), 86.

21. Ibid., 87.

22. Ibid., 89–90.

23. See Norbert Schwarz and Fritz Strack, "Reports of Subjective Well-Being: Judgmental Processes and Their Methodological Implications," in *Well-Being: The Foundations of Hedonic Psychology,* edited by Daniel Kahneman, Ed Diener, and Norbert Schwarz (New York: Russell Sage Foundation, 2003), 61–84, for a discussion of various empirical studies recently conducted.

24. Ibid., 70.

25. Ibid., 64.

26. Ibid., 74.

27. Ibid., 75.

28. Ibid.

CHAPTER SEVEN

Happiness and Morality

The question "Can an immoral person be happy?" has troubled philosophers since the ancient Greeks began thinking about ethics more than two thousand years ago. Historically, philosophers have used happiness as an incentive for people to engage in moral behavior, and they have denied the happiness of anyone failing to live a virtuous life. In contrast, the life-satisfaction view, which identifies happiness with being satisfied with your life, places no restriction on how one achieves satisfaction and, therefore, grants the possibility that the immoralist might be happy.

In this chapter we shall explore the connection between happiness and morality. I begin by presenting the case of the happy immoralist, and I offer a reply to objectors who wish to deny the immoral person's happiness. Then I address the question of whether it is being moral that promotes a person's happiness or merely maintaining the appearance of being moral.

The Happy Immoralist

In the lead article of a symposium featured in the *Journal of Social Philosophy,* Steven M. Cahn claims that an immoral person can achieve happiness. As an illustration, he presents the fictitious example of Fred, a happy immoralist. According to Cahn, Fred has achieved his three most important goals in life: fame, wealth, and a reputation for probity. Nevertheless, he is "treacherous and dishonest."[1] He maintains his reputation for moral uprightness by keeping his immorality secret. Because he has succeeded in doing so, he is satisfied with his life. In short, he is happy.

Fred is not bothered that his happiness is caused by immorality. He is satisfied, though immoral, because being moral is not important to him. His only concern is appearing to be moral, and he has achieved that goal.

Now let us consider several arguments put forth by contemporary philosophers who wish to challenge Cahn's account of Fred's happiness. John Kleinig views happiness as "a recognition that the various parts of one's life are functioning well in a coherent and stable fashion." Kleinig refers to Fred's happiness as "epistemically unsound" because of the way Fred has achieved his goals, and he describes Fred's "path to success" in maintaining happiness as "an extremely perilous one." Kleinig believes that for most of us, "happiness is bound up with living a life very different from Fred's." Kleinig says that "real happiness" is intimately related to "a certain kind of social world" characterized by "trust, truthfulness and respect." Given Fred's values, Kleinig concludes that "at one important level his happiness is chimerical."[2]

Kleinig's objection to Fred's happiness is surprising, given Kleinig's own understanding of happiness. Kleinig identifies happiness with the recognition that "one's important goals are being accomplished, and that one is satisfied with how they are being accomplished."[3] Clearly, Fred meets this condition, for Fred is achieving all his important goals and is exceedingly satisfied with the way his life is going. So why does Kleinig describe Fred's happiness as "epistemically unsound" and "chimerical"?

Kleinig is bothered by the "fragility of Fred's psychosocial world."[4] Fred's happiness is caused by deception and falsehood, but according to Kleinig, "real happiness" is bound up with virtues that Fred's life lacks. This approach introduces an element of objective value into Kleinig's account of happiness. He adds that, in addition to reaching our goals, we must have the right goals.

Jeffrie Murphy shares Kleinig's intuition about the instability of Fred's happiness, and he charges that Fred is attached to "temporal values that are vulnerable," particularly because they are "dependent on the responses of others." According to Murphy, temporal desires leave one "vulnerable to the vicissitudes of fate and fortune and carry only temporary satisfaction," leading to a kind of happiness that is only momentary. Murphy also suspects that Fred's happiness is diminished by the fear of its fragility and that contemplation of future unhappiness would "at the very least pose a serious obstacle to his being fully happy now." Murphy concludes, "When I think of the man described by Cahn, I find that I *pity* him. . . . But why would I pity him if I thought he was truly happy?"[5]

Christopher Gowans also questions Fred's happiness, suspecting Fred is "not only lonely but anxious as well." Although Gowans is willing to acknowledge some diversity among the causes of people's happiness, he believes that "human nature seems to impose some limits on this diversity." Gowans believes that friendship is essential for happiness, and he wonders "whether Fred, while sitting alone watching himself praised on his wide-screen television, ever feels lonely." Gowans suspects that Fred also suffers from anxiety over being exposed, and "since he has no friends, he has no one to whom to express this." Gowans believes that Cahn's example "does not provide us with a convincing case of a happy immoralist," and he concludes that "perhaps Fred is happy in some respects, but we should be most engaged with the respects in which he is probably not."[6]

The first problem with these objections to Cahn's example is that they fail to accurately reflect our common understanding of happiness. Although the ancient Greeks had a tradition of conflating happiness with morality, denying that happiness was attainable by anyone who was not virtuous, the word no longer retains that meaning today. When I say that someone is happy, I am referring to her state of mind. Being happy implies nothing about the value of a person's life independent of her own perceptions. Furthermore, happiness is not the primary or sole reason for action; it is merely one motivation among others. Some people act out of a sense of duty or a desire for excellence, but these concerns may have nothing to do with happiness and provide no guarantee of it.

Fred views his life positively, because he is attaining those goals he deems valuable, yet all three objectors express skepticism over the value of those goals and share the view that Fred's blatant immorality precludes him from happiness. But focusing on what Fred's life lacks is irrelevant to the question of whether he is happy, for if Fred is not bothered by what his life is missing, he need not be dissatisfied. That I would not be happy living your life is no reason to assume that you are not happy living it.

The connection posited by Kleinig between happiness and "a certain kind of social world" may apply to some people, but not to Fred. For people who value being moral, considerations of happiness will clearly be intertwined with morality, for their satisfaction will require living up to their ethical obligations. The mistake is to assume all people share these values. Gowans makes a similar error by assuming that Fred would benefit from genuine friendship. If I am content being alone, having more friends may not increase my happiness. Although friendships, family relationships, and children are all sources of some people's happiness, to others they can become sources of misery.

Returning to the charge that Fred's happiness is unstable, I wonder whose happiness is ever "epistemically sound" or invulnerable to "the vicissitudes of fate and fortune." I believe Fred's happiness is no less secure than anyone else's, for our moral values provide us with little protection against many sources of misery and unhappiness. For example, we can have strong attachments to other people whose health and safety are beyond our control. Likewise, we usually value our health and careers, but no matter how virtuous we are, one or both may fail. The happiness of all people is fragile, although most of us tend not to think about our situations, clinging instead to the false belief that virtue can guard us against evils. In reality, the immoralist's happiness, like the happiness of everyone else, is vulnerable to the vicissitudes of life.

Furthermore, I wonder why Gowans assumes that Fred does not have any friends. After all, Fred is supposed to be a successful immoralist, not an unsuccessful one. Although he is immoral, no one else knows that. On the outside, Fred appears to be kindhearted and caring; people believe he is a virtuous person. Surely, then, Fred is respected by many who consider him a good friend. What distinguishes Fred is not that he has no friends but that he doesn't care whether he has any.

The same sort of misunderstanding leads Murphy to misdiagnose Fred's situation. You may pity Fred because you frown upon his lifestyle; you might prefer to be a more honorable (if less popular) person. Perhaps you are also skeptical about Fred's ability to keep up the charade. You may be worried that Fred's duplicity will be exposed; you may fear the repercussions if his immorality is revealed. But why assume Fred shares your values or anxieties? You might not want happiness that results from immorality, but someone else might. Your moral objection to Fred's lifestyle is a reflection of your own values and says little about the quality of Fred's life.

Thus, none of Cahn's critics presents a compelling argument that challenges Fred's happiness. Those tempted to deny it seek to keep morality and happiness closely tied, because once you recognize their independence, you open the door to the dreaded question, "Why be moral?" If you acknowledge that a person's happiness can come into conflict with the duty to be moral, and you agree that it is rational to pursue one's own happiness, you are forced to acknowledge that behaving immorally could be rational.

Many moral philosophers try to avoid this conclusion by denying that morality and happiness can conflict. They presume that acknowledging reasons for action other than one's moral obligations will diminish the importance of morality or encourage people to take their moral obligations less seriously. However, I believe the solution to the issue is not to deny the immoralist's happiness. The philosopher's attempt to steal back the word *happiness* from the common lexicon and supply it with a philosophical definition does little to improve the prospects for morality and only deepens the chasm between philosophers and ordinary people.

Morality or the Appearance of Morality?

Although happiness and morality are conceptually independent, an empirical correlation exists between a person's moral character and happiness. Because most of us desire to develop and sustain relationships with others who will be more likely to react positively to us if we are kind and trustworthy, being moral enhances our potential for happiness. Alternatively, a person's nastiness and treachery will win few friends.

I am not denying the possibility of the happy tyrant, the happy hermit, or the happy immoralist; however, most of us rely on the goodwill of others in order to be happy. Psychologists studying happiness have found a positive correlation between people's social contacts (including family and friends) and the level of satisfaction with their lives. As psychologist Michael Argyle notes, "In many studies [social relationships] come out as the greatest single source of happiness."[7] Because having a social network is for most people an important source of happiness, almost all of us have an interest in being viewed favorably by others. Acting immorally might result in short-term gains, but in the longer run, it will besmirch our reputations.

Although no controversy surrounds the recognition of an empirical connection between a person's moral character and happiness, a crucial issue often overlooked is whether the benefit to us derives from our being moral or merely appearing to be moral. The virtuous person is bound by her moral obligations and so is unable to capitalize on opportunities to increase happiness through immoral actions. The person who merely appears to be virtuous will enjoy exactly the same advantages in reputation gained by someone who actually is virtuous, but she will be able to exploit situations in which immorality enhances happiness. Thus, what is crucial for maximal happiness is not being moral but appearing to be moral.

To develop this point more fully, consider these four cases: (1) a moral person who appears to be moral, (2) an immoral person who appears to be moral, (3) a moral person who appears to be immoral, and (4) an immoral person who appears to be immoral.

Case (4) is worst for the subject. The blatant immoralist may be able to achieve some short-term gains but once recognized as immoral will be unlikely to be happy, because immoral actions will lead at the very least to social disapproval, if not a jail term.

Case (3), a moral person who appears to be immoral, is almost as bad for promoting happiness. Although the subject can take pride in knowing that she is acting morally, she will nevertheless suffer all the negative consequences associated with being a blatant immoralist. Consider as an example an attorney who, believing that justice requires all those accused of crimes to have competent counsel, agrees to defend a terrorist accused of a murderous bombing. The attorney has no sympathy whatsoever for the deadly attack but does her best in the interest of her client. The public fails to appreciate her position and views her as a terrorist sympathizer. Threats are made against her and her family, and she is eventually forced to give up her practice and move to another locale. She has acted morally and may receive some personal satisfaction from having taken a courageous stand, but because the public views her actions as immoral, she has impaired her happiness, just as she would have had she acted immorally.

Case (1), a moral person who appears to be moral, offers a commonly accepted model for achieving happiness but still has drawbacks. In those circumstances in which happiness depends on acting immorally, the moral person will be forced to sacrifice happiness for the sake of morality. Do such circumstances actually arise? Let us consider an example. Anne is invited to go to a concert that takes place at the same time she is supposed to help some friends paint their apartment. Anne had promised to help her friends paint, but the band is Anne's favorite, and this appearance is their last engagement before they break up. Anne does not want to miss this once-in-a-lifetime opportunity, but her friends would be greatly upset if Anne broke her promise. What should she do?

As a virtuous person, she has no choice but to honor her commitment, thus missing an opportunity that would bring her happiness. If, however, she were not virtuous, she might fabricate a compelling excuse and achieve greater happiness. Some might suppose that Anne's lie would in some way bring her unhappiness, but that assumption, while perhaps comforting, is unwarranted. We could tell a story about how Anne's breaking her promise worked out badly for her and her friends, but we could equally easily tell a story about how the lie worked out well for all of them.

Sometimes the path of morality leads to misery. For example, someone may stop his car to help a stranger fix a flat tire, only to be hit by an oncoming truck. The whistle-blower may as a result of telling the truth be fired, while the politician who refuses to vote against her conscience may thereby forfeit a realistic chance for reelection. In all such cases, the individual's happiness is lost as a result of adhering to moral standards.

In case (2), however, an immoral person who appears to be moral, the subject possesses all the advantages of a reputation for being moral while avoiding the disadvantages of always acting as morality dictates. Such an individual retains the option of acting immorally, whenever greater happiness would result. Admittedly, the person does take a significant risk, because exposure might bring ruin, but by striving to develop a reputation for being moral, and acting immorally only when the payoff is huge and the chances of being caught are small, the crafty immoralist may find more happiness than anyone else.

Faced with this conclusion, many philosophers have been tempted to defuse the problem by focusing on cases of extreme depravity and making the obvious point that such behavior is less preferable than adherence to conventional morality. The more realistic choice that confronts each person, however, is not whether to choose unmitigated evils but whether to do wrong when such action offers a plausible path to happiness. In the end, as we face critical decisions in what may be highly tempting circumstances, how we choose to act will ultimately define who we are as individuals.

Notes

1. Steven M. Cahn, "The Happy Immoralist," *Journal of Social Philosophy* 35 (2004): 1.

2. John Kleinig, "Happiness and Virtue," *Journal of Social Philosophy* 35 (2004): 2.

3. Ibid.

4. Ibid.

5. Jeffrie Murphy, "The Unhappy Immoralist," *Journal of Social Philosophy* 35 (2004): 12–13.

6. Christopher Gowans, "Should Fred Elicit Our Derision or Our Compassion?," *Journal of Social Philosophy* 35 (2004): 15.

7. Michael Argyle, "Causes and Correlates of Happiness," in *Well-Being: The Foundations of Hedonic Psychology,* edited by Daniel Kahneman, Ed Diener, and Norbert Schwarz (New York: Russell Sage Foundation, 2003), 362.

CHAPTER EIGHT

The Pursuit of Happiness

According to the life-satisfaction view, happiness is a state of satisfaction that implies nothing about the value of a person's life independent of her own perceptions. A person's happiness is proportional to how positively she views her life: the more favorable her impression, the happier she will be. But if happiness amounts to personal satisfaction, isn't it achieved simply by seeking to fulfill immediate desires? Doesn't granting people first-person authority with respect to their happiness preclude giving them advice?

I believe such concerns are unwarranted. Satisfaction does not render useless the value of advice, for present satisfaction does not ensure future satisfaction. A person's happiness attained unwisely may be only short-term, leading to unhappiness in the longer run. Happiness is also a degree notion. One may be happy, yet her level of satisfaction may be at the lower end of the scale. Thus, advising people about their choices can call attention to the shortsightedness of their goals or the limited intensity of their satisfaction. We don't have to deny that a person is happy in order to make suggestions about changes that could ensure future or greater happiness.

Consider Ted, who frequently skips school to hang out with his friends. His problem is that his happiness is only short-term. Eventually, he is going to fail out of school, severely limiting his prospects. Although he is satisfied now, he is jeopardizing his future happiness, trading it for some short-term pleasure. Granting that Ted is happy does not require us to approve of his lifestyle, nor does it preclude our providing him advice. We can seek to change

131

his present behavior by appealing to his future prospects. We can also increase his chances for greater happiness by offering him strategies for increasing happiness that others have found effective.

Such strategies can take two forms. To distinguish them, consider Jaime, whose goal is to gain acceptance into a doctoral program in psychology. She has already applied to numerous departments but has been rejected by them all. Jaime is now unhappy and seeks help. One strategy consistent with the life-satisfaction view is to search for new means of achieving her goals. Therefore, we might suggest that Jaime apply to less prestigious schools, where she has a better chance of being accepted.

For that strategy to be effective, however, alternative means must be available that have not yet been tried. The strategy cannot help the person who clings to unreachable goals or faces insurmountable obstacles. For example, an aspiring actress or professional athlete may lack the talent needed for success. Such people are not guilty of lack of effort; rather, their goals are beyond their grasp, and seeking to achieve their dreams will lead only to unhappiness.

Other people suffer from bad luck. Consider a tennis player, moments away from winning her first championship, who suffers an injury that forces her to forfeit the match. She tries to compete again, but her injury affects her ability to play the game competitively. She never gets close to winning another tournament because her injury has essentially destroyed her career. As long as she holds on to the dream of being a professional tennis player, she will be unhappy.

A person's happiness, however, is not static. It is affected by not only external events but also internal changes in an individual's preferences. Recognizing people as dynamic beings, who are able to change their desires, goals, and values, enables us to appeal to a second strategy to alleviate unhappiness. Rather than seeking to change our external conditions, we can try to change our goals, modifying them or abandoning them altogether.

Let us imagine that Jaime, our aspiring graduate student, has tried every available means of achieving her goal. Unfortunately, she still has not been accepted into any doctoral programs, because her record in psychology is not strong enough. What else can she do? She can rethink why she likes psychology and then try to develop an alternative goal that is attainable. Perhaps she was drawn to the subject because she likes helping people. She might find professions that are equally fulfilling but do not require attending graduate school.

In her fixation on becoming a psychologist, she had ignored these possibilities, but once she abandons her unrealistic goals and replaces them with more attainable ones, she may become satisfied with her life and achieve happiness.

One important implication of the life-satisfaction view is that each person controls her own happiness. People often see a gap between what they want and what they have and, believing this gap insurmountable, fall into despair. But goals can be altered, thereby creating new avenues toward satisfaction.

However, dissatisfaction is not always bad. If a person does not work up to her potential, or if alternative means for achieving goals can be found, then dissatisfaction is appropriate and can even be helpful. In such cases, experiencing unhappiness can motivate one to increased effort and greater resilience. Consider Leah, who receives a low grade on an important exam she expected to ace. She sees herself as an excellent student, but this exam was more challenging than she had anticipated, and she was overconfident about her mastery of the material. So the night before the exam when her friends asked her to go to the movies, she joined them rather than spending the extra time studying. As a result, she received a low grade and is unhappy.

Leah's unhappiness, however, does not result from desiring an unattainable goal. On the contrary, she is unhappy because she knows her aim was attainable. Had she studied sufficiently, she would have done well. Leah's dissatisfaction is reasonable, and, furthermore, her unhappiness may be good for her, because it may keep her from being overconfident in the future. Feeling dissatisfied need not imply viewing a situation as hopeless, nor must it condemn one to despair about the perceived gap between what we want and what we have. Instead, unhappiness can prevent a person from becoming complacent and inspire a search for new ways to achieve success.

Sometimes, however, what we seek is not within the realm of practical possibility. In such cases, dissatisfaction is self-destructive. Rather than motivating a person to try harder, the dissatisfaction results in hopelessness. In such instances, the life-satisfaction view implies that changing one's perspective can make happiness achievable.

One final point. Suppose someone asks you whether your life is happy. The answer depends on whether you look "upward," comparing your life to how good it might have been, or whether you look " downward," comparing your life to how bad it might have become. Looking upward is apt to lead you to say you are not so happy, because of the gap between your actual achieve-ments and an ideal life. But if you look downward, you are likely to report in-creased happiness, considering your life in comparison to far worse possibilities. Although all the external features of your life remain the same, whether you compare your life to better or worse alternatives impacts your happiness. In other words, focusing on what you have achieved rather than on what you have failed to achieve can dispel dissatisfaction. Here is another way, according to the life-satisfaction view, that achieving happiness lies within your power.

These insights are reminiscent of the outlook of the Stoics, whose philos-ophy we discussed in Chapter 2. Recall their emphasis on changing one's mind rather than trying to change the world, for our minds are within our control, whereas events in the world are not. The Stoic outlook fits well with the life-satisfaction view of happiness.

Conclusion

Happiness transcends the barriers of race, religion, and culture. I may not un-derstand the values of your society or share your language, customs, or beliefs, yet knowing you are happy tells me something important about your life.

I was struck by this power of happiness while traveling in East Africa, where I had the opportunity to visit a traditional Masai village in Kenya. Prior to the visit, our tour guide gave us a brief cultural lesson on the Masai. We were told that their lifestyle is nomadic and pastoral, revolving around their cattle. The Masai live in small huts made out of cow dung, and they sleep on beds made from cowhides. The cattle also provide food for the Masai, whose diet consists of cow meat, milk, and blood. The wealth of the Masai is measured in terms of their cattle, and to the Masai, amassing material possessions other than cattle is useless.

Our guide gave us a firm warning: "Do not feel sorry for these people. They are happy." Initially, this view was hard to understand. My initial reaction prior to meeting the Masai was, "Sure, *he* says they're happy, but they live in such poverty. How can they be happy?" My tendency was to focus on the Ma-sai's lack of basic amenities and their unawareness of modern technology.

After visiting the Masai, however, I came to share our guide's outlook, for their satisfaction with their lives was obvious. They clearly took a lot of pride in their traditional lifestyle and were eager to share their customs with our group. The clothes of the Masai consisted of simple robes, but they were beautiful, their bright colors standing out dramatically against the arid, dusty landscape. Although the Masai lacked even such basic amenities as plumbing and electricity, most were educated and sent their children to school.

An outsider might be tempted to pity these people, as I initially did before meeting them, but this is a mistake. Although their lifestyle is different from ours, so too are their desires, and all of their needs are being met. They are not suffering, and their lives are filled with enjoyment. In short, the Masai are happy.

The life-satisfaction view can explain the happiness of people regardless of how different their lifestyles may be. It explains why the Masai, who possess so little, are nevertheless happy, as well as why some wealthy people in our own society, who possess so much, may still be deeply unhappy. Happiness is a state of mind. If over the course of your life you fail to appreciate what you have, you will never be happy. But if you can find satisfaction in your situation, whatever it may be, then happiness will be yours.

APPENDIX:
THE EXPERIENCE MACHINE

There is a well-known thought experiment that many theorists believe disproves hedonism. However, I shall argue that it does not present a serious reason to reject hedonism, and I discuss two replies the hedonist could offer. The objection comes from the prominent contemporary philosopher Robert Nozick, who poses a thought experiment involving an experience machine. Nozick asks us to imagine a machine that can give a person any pleasant experience she desires. By stimulating your brain, neuropsychologists can make it seem as though you are having certain experiences, even though you are really just lying unconscious in a machine. From your perspective, being hooked up to the machine will feel no different from when you actually have the experience, because your brain will be put into the exact same mental state you would be in if you were having that particular experience.

We are also told the neuropsychologists have a huge library of desirable experiences, and you are free to choose whatever interests you. For instance, perhaps you have always wanted to be an astronaut; you could choose to experience what it's like to float in space or walk on the moon. Suppose you love the arts; you could be a prima ballerina or sing an aria in your favorite opera. Or maybe you love sports; in that case, you might choose to play on a professional team or have the experience of being a team owner. You will be able to choose all of the experiences you desire for the next two years, after which they will wake you up and let you choose again. Nozick tells us that other people can plug in too, so you should not feel any pressure to "stay in reality" in order to be with your friends or relatives.

The question that interests Nozick is whether you should plug into this machine and preprogram your life's experiences. Would plugging in be good for you? Nozick's reply is a resounding no, and he offers three reasons. First, he says that "we want to *do* certain things, and not just have the experience of doing them." For instance, I choose to volunteer at a local soup kitchen because I think it is important to help people who are less fortunate. I am not interested in merely having "the experience" of volunteering or falsely believing that I've volunteered. I want to actually volunteer, which cannot be done by plugging into the machine. Second, Nozick says that "we want to be a certain way, to be a certain sort of person." But when we are hooked up to the machine, we are nothing more than an indeterminate blob, floating in a tank. Nozick suggests that hooking up to the machine makes it hard to determine who you are as an individual, and he views it as a kind of suicide. Finally, Nozick argues that "plugging into an experience machine limits us to man-made reality, to a world no deeper or more important than that which people can construct."[1] He suggests that many people wish to leave open the possibility of contact with something of deeper significance, which is yet another reason we should not hook up to the experience machine.

Nozick concludes that our refusal to plug in teaches us something important about what matters to us, for it proves we value more than our own experiences and prefer to live our lives rather than have machines do it for us. James Griffin, another prominent contemporary philosopher, agrees with Nozick. As he explains, "I prefer, in important areas of my life, bitter truth to comfortable delusion." Griffin offers a variation of Nozick's objection: Suppose highly skilled actors are able to provide you with the illusion that you are well loved and respected. Would you want to live such a life? Griffin's reply is also no, because "I should prefer the relatively bitter diet of their authentic reactions. And I should prefer it not because it would be morally better, or aesthetically better, or more noble, but because it would make for a better life for me to live."[2]

Nozick's thought experiment challenges hedonism about happiness, because plugging into the experience machine enables you to enjoy the most pleasant, desirable experiences while avoiding all of the pain and misery that are associated with reality. If happiness is equivalent to pleasure, then plugging in should make you very happy. But according to Nozick, most people would not want to plug into the machine even though most people desire happiness. Our reluctance to plug in is taken as evidence that the person in the machine is not actually happy, even though she is undergoing experiences of pleasure. Therefore, we are to conclude that the hedonist must be wrong about the nature of happiness.

I see two problems with Nozick's thought experiment, both of which redeem hedonism. First, even if people refuse to plug into the machine, their reasons may involve other values, such as considerations related to morality, religion, or well-being, which have nothing to do with happiness. Therefore, one cannot assume a refusal to plug in is evidence against hedonism about happiness.[3] Second, I disagree with Nozick's intuition about how people will react to plugging into the experience machine, especially when you consider the prevalence of escapist behavior within our society. If Nozick is wrong and people do choose the experience machine, the thought experiment does not undermine hedonism. I shall discuss each problem further and then address Griffin's objection.

Let's begin with the first problem. Suppose Sally refuses to plug into the experience machine, but we know that Sally wants to be happy. Does Sally's refusal imply the experience machine cannot make one happy? Not necessarily, because Sally's refusal may simply reflect other values she deems more important than happiness. For instance, Sally may be morally opposed to happiness that is caused by deception, or she may believe her religion prohibits her from hooking up to the machine. Although both reasons might cause Sally to refuse plugging into the experience machine, neither implies anything about whether the machine actually causes happiness. Consider a parallel example. Joan is a vegetarian who is morally opposed to eating meat and hunting for sport. But she cannot deny the happiness of carnivores and hunters, simply because she finds the source of their happiness morally objectionable. Therefore, we cannot count refusal to plug into the experience machine as evidence against hedonism, for their refusals may involve reasons that are entirely independent of happiness.

Next, let us turn to the second problem with Nozick's argument. I am not convinced that many people (besides professional philosophers) would be strongly opposed to plugging into the machine. Just look at how we choose to spend our free time: we read novels and watch movies, play virtual reality video games, participate in re-creations of famous battles, attend Renaissance festivals, and visit theme parks like Walt Disney World and Colonial Williamsburg. This list contains only a fraction of the benign and relatively harmless ways in which we seek an escape from our ordinary experiences. Perhaps even more compelling is the prevalence of harmful methods of escape many people seek, such as the use of psychedelic drugs, narcotics, prescription pain medication, and various other illegal substances. All of this escapist behavior suggests we may be more likely to be receptive to the experience machine than Nozick is willing to acknowledge.

Now let me emphasize the limits of my argument: even if the experience machine is a huge success, we cannot conclude anything definitive about whether it causes happiness. The reasons in favor of plugging in will be just as varied as the reasons against it, and they too will likely involve considerations that are entirely independent of happiness. My point is that you cannot make any assumptions about the nature of happiness (and whether it is equivalent to pleasure) based on people's reactions to the experience machine. Therefore, the experience machine thought experiment does not present us with a reason to reject hedonism.

Finally, I would like to briefly address Griffin's argument. According to Griffin, we should prefer reality to delusion, because it makes our lives better for us to live. Considering the research within psychology on cognitive biases, I am skeptical of how well any of us apprehends reality and whether we are worse off for the delusion. Consider the "optimism bias," which leads us to overestimate the likelihood of positive events and underestimate the likelihood of negative ones. Studies have shown this bias is pervasive and affects a wide range of people. Students overestimate their grades, newlyweds overestimate the length of their marriages, financial analysts overestimate corporate earnings, and smokers underestimate their risk of disease.[4]

"Illusory superiority" is another cognitive bias that causes people to overestimate their positive qualities and abilities (and to underestimate the negative) when compared to others. This bias has been found to affect judgments in a wide range of areas, including intelligence, performance on a specific task, academic ability, job performance, and driving skills. Illusory superiority also occurs in social contexts, with subjects overestimating their own leadership skills, ability to get along with others, popularity, and relationship satisfaction when compared to others.[5]

The prevalence of cognitive biases suggests that most people apprehend reality through rose-colored glasses, for we tend to see things as being much better than they actually are, and we remain optimistic about the future even when the "facts" suggest otherwise. However, psychologists have found a small group of people who do not suffer from cognitive biases; they consistently rate their abilities accurately, and they are not overly optimistic about the future. The only problem is that these people, who appear to have a much better apprehension of reality, also suffer from moderate depression. Therefore, the empirical research suggests that happy people are likely deluded about many aspects of their lives, while those who are not deceived are moderately depressed. Now Griffin may prefer depressive realism to deceptive happiness, but that tells us only about Griffin's own preferences—that he values truth more than happiness. His refusal, like the vegetarian who prefers not to eat meat, tells us very little about the nature of happiness.

Notes

1. Robert Nozick, "The Experience Machine," in *Happiness: Classic and Contemporary Readings in Philosophy*, edited by Steven M. Cahn and Christine Vitrano (New York: Oxford University Press, 2008), 236, 237.

2. James Griffin, *Well-Being* (New York: Oxford University Press, 1986), 9.

3. Jean Kazez considers an interesting alternative version of Nozick's "experience machine" thought experiment in her book *The Weight of Things* (Oxford: Blackwell, 2007). Rather than asking us whether we would want to plug in, she has us suppose we are already plugged in, so that everything we are presently experiencing has been preprogrammed. Kazez prefers this alternative to the original version, because she acknowledges that the "refusal to hook up is not actually so easy to interpret" and that there may be other reasons for our refusal besides the quality of our lives or our own happiness (52).

4. David Armor and Shelley Taylor, "When Predictions Fail: The Dilemma of Unrealistic Optimism," in *Heuristics and Biases: The Psychology of Intuitive Judgment*, edited by Thomas Gilovich, Griffin Dale, and Daniel Kahneman (Cambridge: Cambridge University Press, 2002).

5. Vera Hoorens, "Self-Enhancement and Superiority Biases in Social Comparison," *European Review of Social Psychology* 4 (1993): 113–139; J. Suls, K. Lemos, and H. L. Stewart, "Self-Esteem, Construal, and Comparisons with the Self, Friends, and Peers," *Journal of Personality and Social Psychology* 82 (2002): 252–261.

INDEX